Power Chess for Kids

Charles Hertan

Power Chess for Kids

Learn How to Think Ahead and Become
One of the Best Players in Your School

New In Chess 2011

© 2011 New In Chess
Published by New In Chess, Alkmaar, The Netherlands
www.newinchess.com

Photos: New In Chess Archives, Photo of the author (page 155): Jerry Rubin

Cover design: Volken Beck
Artwork: Zander Dekker
Supervisor: Peter Boel
Proofreading: René Olthof
Production: Anton Schermer

ISBN: 978-90-5691-330-4

Contents

Meet the Main Characters. 7

Introduction
Three Skills You Need to Be One of the Best Players in Your School . . 9

Chapter 1
Four Tricks to Help You Think 1.5 Power Moves Ahead. 15

Chapter 2
Forks. 43

Chapter 3
Pins 77

Chapter 4
Skewers. 119

Chapter 5
Interference Moves 137

Chess Terms 151

About the Author 155

Index of Players. 157

Meet the Main Characters

Four fun characters in this book will help you learn **power moves** and think ahead like a pro:

Zort from Zugzwang

Zort is a teenaged computer from the planet Zugzwang. His favorite hobbies are chess, facebook and googling. Zort thinks his planet is boring, because only computers live there, they all look kind of alike, and they aren't much fun. Zort was googling images of kids playing on planet Earth, and fell in love with these exotic creatures. When he found out I was writing a kids' book, he wanted to help. As luck would have it, there was one way he could help a lot. Thinking two moves ahead is hard for us humans, so I thought it was unfair that many kids' books expect you to play through 5-move long variations! Hard for us, but easy for computers, who have a big advantage: a perfect picture of the board in their 'minds', after every move! Zort had a great idea: when a variation in the book is longer than two or three moves, he will use his computer **board sight** to show you the key positions.

The Dinosaurs

'The Dinosaurs' is a nickname for players in the first great chess tournaments, from the 1850's to the 1890's. Why do I call them that? Well, besides being old, they played like dinosaurs: awkward and crude, but also deadly! They didn't like draws, so they went for the kill every game, even in bad positions. This made for exciting chess, full of tactics and great power moves. At first I worried some kids might find these old games boring, but Zort reminded me that most kids love dinosaurs. Plus, think how cool it is that you can look in a book or database and find games that were played 150 years ago! Wouldn't it be *awesome* if one of your games was in a book in the year 2159? If you study and practice hard enough, it really might be!

Power Chess Kids

Lots of kids' chess books don't answer the questions kids really want to know! So you, the chess kids of the world, have a voice in this book to make comments and ask typical questions that kids of different ages ask when I teach these power moves.

The Chess Professor

The chess professor will help answer kids' questions and give you important winning tips.

Algebraic Notation

8	a8	b8	c8	d8	e8	f8	g8	h8
7	a7	b7	c7	d7	e7	f7	g7	h7
6	a6	b6	c6	d6	e6	f6	g6	h6
5	a5	b5	c5	d5	e5	f5	g5	h5
4	a4	b4	c4	d4	e4	f4	g4	h4
3	a3	b3	c3	d3	e3	f3	g3	h3
2	a2	b2	c2	d2	e2	f2	g2	h2
1	a1	b1	c1	d1	e1	f1	g1	h1
	a	b	c	d	e	f	g	h

The files are labeled a-h, and the ranks are labeled 1-8. So each square has its own name. The pieces are described as follows (pawns do not get a symbol, so if you see '1.e4' that means White's first move was pawn e2 to e4):

Knight   = ♘
Bishop   = ♗
Rook   = ♖
Queen   = ♕
King   = ♔

We also use the following symbols:

Check   = +
Checkmate   = #
Capture   = x
Castles kingside = 0-0   queenside = 0-0-0
Good move   = !
Bad move   = ?

While many kids' books use simplified diagrams, this book has the same diagrams used in adult chess books, which shows some additional information which is fun to know! The square next to each diagram indicates which colour is to move. Above each diagram you'll see a label like this:

Del Pozo-Jauregui, Lima 1959

The first word (**Del Pozo**) is the last name of the player of the white pieces. **Jauregui** played black. This way you get to know the names of many famous players. They are followed by the city or country, and the year, in which the game was played. At the end of the game, the symbol **0-1** means Black won the game (or had a winning advantage), **1-0** means White won, and ½-½ means a draw.

Introduction

Three Skills You Need to Be One of the Best Players in Your School

What are the first three things you should study to become a tiger at chess? The list might surprise you:

1. Know the **basic checkmates**.
2. Learn the key **master tactics** for checkmate and winning material.
3. Work on **thinking one and a half moves ahead**.

In this book we will work mostly on numbers two and three, but you will improve your skills on #1 too. Why doesn't this book focus more on basic checkmates? Well, there are lots of good kids' books on checkmate, but not many that teach all the power move tactics that help you think ahead and win games.

Here's another secret:
Learning master tactics is the best way to sharpen *all* three basic skills.

How can learning tactics help me think ahead?

Good question! Master tactics help you think ahead in two ways. You learn to recognize patterns that help you find winning moves quickly. Then you start calculating to see how you can make these patterns work in your games.

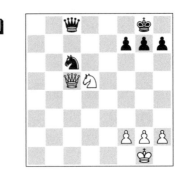

White can win this position, but only if he knows master tactics and sees **1.5 power moves** ahead! ('one move' in chess means your move, plus your opponent's reply. Your move only is called a 'half move'). Most kids in your school wouldn't know what to do in the diagram. If they've studied pins, they might look at 1.♘e7+ or 1.♘b4, to attack the pinned black knight. But 1.♘e7+?? loses to 1...♘xe7 protecting the queen, and if 2.♕xe7 ♕c1+ mates on the back rank. 1.♘b4 is a little better, but Black can escape the pin with, for example, 1...♕e8!, threatening the same mate.

After reading this book, you will be able to find the winning move in about five seconds: **1.♕xc6! ♕xc6 2.♘e7+** regains the queen and keeps an extra knight.

To find this, you only need to see 1.5 power moves ahead – your move, your opponent's best answer, and your winning second play. But most kids wouldn't even consider 1.♕xc6! because it gives the queen. Knowledge of master tactics helps you find this winning pattern easily, by thinking – 'If only I could get rid of his knight, my knight could fork his king and queen. Hey, what if I just take it! Then if he takes back, I still have the win!'

The ability to recognize the **fork trick** by calculating ahead is the only possible way to win this even position, unless your opponent makes a terrible mistake!

That's pretty cool, but what's a power move?

A **power move** is a winning master tactic that requires thinking ahead – one and a half moves or even a bit more. When you start finding these strong moves in your games, you will be a very dangerous player.

What's so great about thinking 1.5 moves ahead? My friend says he can see *ten* moves ahead!

Well, kids say lots of things when they're trying to impress their friends, you know, like 'my dad once swallowed a whole alligator!' But... that's just silly.

The great Hungarian grandmaster Richard Réti once admitted that he usually looked only two moves ahead! When kids say they see five moves ahead, what they're really saying is 'I see the next five moves I'd like to play in my dreams, if the other guy rolls over and plays dead!'

But when a grandmaster says he sees two moves ahead, he means he sees the best moves for *both* sides. That's much harder than it sounds! Consider this: in the first one and a half moves of a game, there are close to 10,000 different possibilities!!

OMG! Then how can *anyone* find the best 1.5 moves?

When you get better, you will learn to weed out 'silly' moves and just consider a few important ones. Studying master tactics helps a lot, teaching you which **power moves** to look out for. A master always checks for these winning tactics first. If he can't find one, he looks for a good *positional* move to improve his pieces a little bit.

So how far ahead do most kids *really* analyze?

A chess teacher from England named Richard James tested a whole bunch of kids from different school chess clubs, from young kids to older teenagers. He gave them many tactical positions to solve, and this is what he found:

Most kids think just one half of a move ahead. They only see what *they* want to do! Mr. James calls this kind of thinking, 'I go there, then I go there...' because it leaves out something very important: the opponent's best answer!

Michal Scheichenost-Daniel Obdrzalek, Morava U-12, 2008

This position is from a kids' tournament. White achieved a totally won position, but understandably, he got mixed up. He wanted to hang onto his knight without leaving his bishop unprotected, so he thought he had the perfect solution: **1.♘xc4??**. But poor Michal was using Mr. James' 'I go there, then I go there' thinking, and forgot to calculate Black's most forcing reply, **1...♕d1#!** (I bet you saw that one coming!).

How would a master have played it? Well, trying to hang onto everything with 1.♕e3 or 1.♕a5 is OK, but after 1...c3! he will still have to give up one of his pieces to avoid back rank mate. After considering a few purposeful options, a master would find 1.0-0! ♕xd2 2.♕xc4, returning one of the pieces to remove all danger and reach an easily won endgame with the extra bishop and passed a-pawn.

I'm still not sure about your list of the three things I need to become a powerful chess player. What about studying openings and endgames?

Well, those are important too, but you need to learn master tactics first.

Power moves will help you win in all stages of the game! Many kids place much too much importance on openings.

In the great Soviet School of chess, students studied only master tactics and endgames for the first year! If you learn a few basic opening principles like developing quickly and controlling the center, and learn the few most important basic endgame checkmates, you will still be one of the best players in your school if you practice thinking 1.5 power moves ahead.

I promise!

Adventure and Sportsmanship

Chess is the greatest game on earth! It challenges your mind and is played by kids and grown-ups all over the world. Winning is awesome, but it's also very important to work on having a great attitude as a chess player! Remember to enjoy playing, practice good sportsmanship, and be willing to experiment and play fearlessly!

The funny thing is, working on these qualities will actually make you a better player. When you enjoy the beauty and complexity of the game, you think more clearly! Practicing **good sportsmanship** is the right thing to do, but it also lets you learn from your opponent by asking what he was thinking after the game. Proper sportsmanship means always being courteous to your opponent. When you lose, you should shake hands and say 'good game', even if you're feeling very frustrated. Nobody likes losing, but it's important to learn to get over your losses quickly, and not worry about them. Sometimes the other guy just plays better than us, or we don't play our best, but if you keep practicing and trying new skills, you *will* become a better player! There is no chess player on earth who didn't have to lose a lot of games, in order to learn important lessons and keep improving.

Playing **adventurous chess** will teach you how to attack, and make you improve faster. Many kids are too afraid to lose, so they don't develop their tactical skills! If you see a good attacking move, but aren't sure if it works, try it! Remember, the goal of a chess game is checkmate, not just protecting all your pieces! Brave play is often best, and it pressures your opponent into making mistakes. Even if it doesn't work out, you'll be learning more about what kind of attacks succeed in different positions.

Whatever happens, keep playing and having fun! Before you know it, you'll start seeing great moves you never thought of before! If your main opponent is too hard or too easy, try finding a practice friend closer to your own strength. Winning every game against someone is kind of boring and doesn't teach you much; but losing every game is also boring and discouraging. Computers are good training partners, but human competition is the best! If you don't have friends who give you a good match, try joining a local chess club or playing online. Chess teaches us something that's very true about everything in life: you can't get good at anything by giving up, but if you like playing and keep sticking with it, you *will* get good!

Chapter 1

Four Tricks to Help You Think 1.5 Power Moves Ahead

So what else do I need to know to start learning power moves?

Ready? Here are the Four Crucial Tricks which will help you find all the winning master tactics in the rest of the book:
1. You must know the **Values of the Pieces**, and always use them in your games to figure out when tactics work!
2. Learn the **Quick Count** method to figure out if a complicated trade is a good deal.
3. & 4. Learn the two easiest ways to think 1.5 power moves ahead:
Takes Takes Bang! and **Check Moves Bang!**

Power Trick #1:

Know and Use The Values of the Pieces

Here's what the pieces are worth:
Queen = 9 Points
Rook = 5
Bishop or Knight = 3
Pawn = 1

The King is priceless; if you lose him you lose the game. But to show what a good attacker he can be when there are few pieces left, and it's safe enough for him to come out, the ♔ is given an attacking value of about 3.5 points.

Many of you probably learned these piece values in a lesson or at a club; but even kids who *know* the values often forget how important it is to use them! What good is having a great tool, if you just let it sit in your toolbox?

The first thing a master does when he looks at a position is to count the material on the board using these simple values. You must also do this to become a strong player! If you don't know whose pieces are worth more, you probably can't tell who has the advantage. If you don't know who has the advantage, it's hard to find the best moves! A key to finding power moves is to use the values during your calculations, to figure out who comes out ahead.

Are these piece values really accurate? The answer is yes. To decide if an unusual trade is a good deal, you can pretty much rely on the piece count. So, for instance, a knight or bishop really is worth about 3 pawns; a rook, bishop and pawn (5+3+1) are about equal to a queen; and a knight and 2 pawns balance a rook. As you get really good, you will learn some fine points about these values; for instance, in the endgame a rook and pawn often balance or sometimes beat a bishop and knight, but earlier in the game the bishop and knight usually have more attacking power. That's why kids should avoid this common mistake:

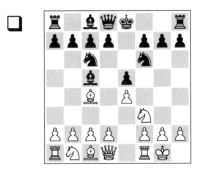

 Both sides have played very good moves so far, developing their pieces toward the center with no wasted ('silly') moves. But when kids start thinking about attacking, they often go a little crazy here with 1.♘g5? 0-0! 2.♘xf7 ♖xf7 3.♗xf7+ ♔xf7.

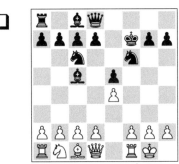

Position after 3...♔xf7

Thanks Zort! White thinks he got a good deal because he took a strong rook. But first, count! White gave up a knight and bishop for rook and pawn, six points each. But look what he did to his poor position, trading his two most active pieces for Black's just-developed rook. Before the trade, White had an equal number of pieces developed and it was his move. Now Black has two more pieces out. (White's castling counts as a developing move.) Black's great knight and bishop have more attacking power at this stage than the white rook, so Black has a big advantage.

So the rule is: **always count the values**, and never give up material without a good reason! You've probably noticed that computers *love* to gobble up material, right Zort?

Oh, yes! If you give me your pawns, I'll eat them all day long! We computers only give up material for something even better, like checkmate. Listen to the professor and count the values of the pieces in *every* position.

You like eating pawns? Eww! I'll take pizza any day.

Use the Values: Exercise

Who's ahead in material? What should White do?

Use the Values: Solution

Del Pozo-Jauregui, Lima 1959

In this really weird position, White has 4 minor pieces for a queen, a 12 to 9 advantage! Even better, he has a great attack: **1.♗d8+! ♔h5 2.♕h8+** and Black resigned because 2...♕h6 3.♗f7+ wins a queen and even mates after the forced 3...♕gg6 4.♕xe5+ ♕hg5 5.♕xg5#.

Power Trick #2: The 'Quick Count'

How to See Far Ahead and Figure Out If You (or Your Opponent) Can Win A Piece

Here's another key tool pros use all the time to figure out combinations. There are many situations in chess where you attack a piece a whole bunch of times, and he defends it a bunch. How can you figure out who's winning, without having to calculate in your head, 'I take him, he takes me, then I take him, he takes me, takes, takes, takes...' It can get confusing pretty fast!

Apsenieks-Raud, Buenos Aires 1939

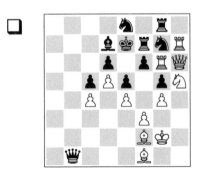

Does White threaten 1.♘xg7?

White has just played his knight from g3 to h5. Here's the question: can White take the g7 knight next move (if Black doesn't stop him), or does Black have enough defenders? While a strong player could see all the captures in his head, it would be easy for him to get mixed up and make a mistake.

OMG! All those captures look so confusing!

Don't worry! I used to feel the same way, until I learned this important trick. Luckily for all of us humans, there's a much easier way to calculate captures:

The Quick Count! Here's how it works:

First: Count how many white pieces attack the ♘g7:

2 rooks, knight and queen make 4 attackers.

Second: Count how many black pieces defend the knight:

2 rooks + 1 knight= 3 defenders.

Okay, now here's the quick count rule: **In order to win his piece, you must have at least one more attacker than he has defenders.** So if it were your move here, you would win the ♘g7 because you have one more attacker – four against three.

This is a great rule that will save you tons of time and help you figure out tricky positions. It's like you just saw 3.5 moves ahead in a few seconds!

Unfortunately, like most rules, there's one important exception you must understand, or it could cost you your queen!

The **Key Exception to the Quick Count Rule** is this:

Your most valuable piece must be able to wait until the last capture.

For instance, in the last diagram, if it was your move and you played **1.♕xg7+??** that would be ridiculous, right? Instead of winning the knight, you would lose your queen for a knight after 1...♘xg7!

By starting instead with 1.♘xg7 and saving the queen recapture for last, you win the ♘g7 for free. The problem is that in some positions, you can't save your best piece for the last recapture, because it's in the way of one of your other pieces.

Aagaard-McNab, Oakham 2000

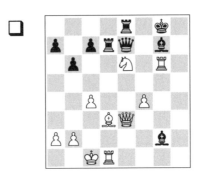

Look at this position won by my friend GM Aagaard of Denmark. Black is rely-ing on White's pinned knight to save him after 1.♖xg7+? ♕xg7 2.♘xg7 ♖xe3 (although White probably still wins after 3.♗h7+), but after **1.♕g3!** Black re-signed immediately. His bishops are both attacked, but what if he moved the one on g2, say **1...♗b7?** Now if you only use the quick count, it seems the ♗g7 is protected: you have 3 attackers, he has 3 defenders (including the ♔). But this is the exception! The black queen is in the way of his rook, and must 'go first' after **2.♖xg7+ ♕xg7 3.♘xg7**.

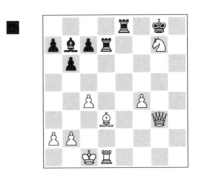

Instead of being equal, Black has lost the queen for just a rook, and is com-pletely lost after **3...♖xg7 4.♕h4**.

Here's the good news: this is the *only* type of exception to the Quick Count Rule. As long as you don't have to start with your stronger pieces, you can al-ways use this rule to figure out if you can take a piece, or if your piece needs more protection.

The Quick Count Rule works just as well for the *defender*. How can you tell if your piece has enough protection?

You already know that among pieces of equal value, the taker needs one more attacker than the defender to win a piece. The other side of the equation is this:

To protect a piece, you must have an *equal* number of defenders as he has attackers (and not have to use your strongest piece too early, like Black did in the last position).

Suppose you're White here, and need to figure out if your d5 pawn is protected. Just do a quick count – you have four defenders (♕b3, ♘c3, ♘f4, ♗f3) and he has four attackers (♘f6, ♘b6, ♖d7, and ♕d8 backing up the rook). Your defenders equal his attackers, and your queen doesn't have to go first, so the pawn is protected!

Don't believe me? Let's calculate it out: Black plays 1...♘fxd5? 2.♘fxd5 ♘xd5 3.♘xd5 ♖xd5 4.♗xd5 (or 4.♕xd5).

Black is very sorry he didn't use the Quick Count! Black has dropped a rook, and if 4...♕xd5?? 5.♕xd5 gets the queen! As this example shows, the defender only needs an equal number of pieces to hold his material, because he goes second and gets the last laugh.

So the quick count tells you that White's d5 pawn is protected, and Black needs to consider forcing moves like 1...g5 or 1...♗h6 in the first diagram, in order to chase away one of White's defenders and try to regain White's extra pawn.

Wow, I get it! Four attackers versus three defenders: I win! Two attackers against two defenders: my piece is protected! That's easier than I thought.

Right, it really is! The only hard part is having good board sight (like Zort) and making sure you notice *all* the chessmen attacking and defending the piece.
And don't forget the key exception! Make sure you can save your best piece for the last capture.

You keep talking about 'board sight'! What do you mean, exactly?

I'm glad you asked! Good **board sight** means keeping track in your head of where all the pieces are, and what they can do, even when you're thinking ahead 1.5 power moves or more.

Developing good board sight is like learning to ride a bicycle. When you first start, you try hard but still stumble and fall like crazy. But with lots of practice you get the hang of it, and it becomes automatic. Good board sight mostly comes from playing as many games as you can and studying power moves, but it certainly helps to try hard, and be alert! Once you decide on a good move, don't make it right away: take one more look around to see if you're missing a key move that one of your pieces, or the opponent's, can make.

The Quick Count: Exercises

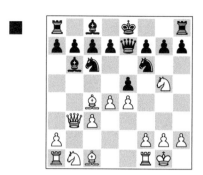

Is White threatening to regain his pawn on f7? How should Black defend?

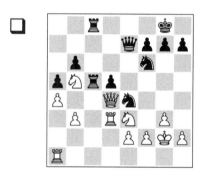

Should White capture the pawn on d5? If not, what's his best plan?

The Quick Count: Solutions

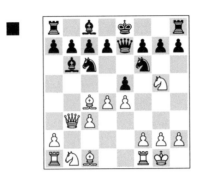

White has 3 attackers of f7 (♘, ♕+♗) vs. 2 defenders (♚+♕) so if it were his move, he could play 1.♗xf7+ with advantage. Black's best defense is 1...0-0! adding a third defender (the rook) to the ♘f7, while also improving his position.

A. Grigoryan-Bocharev, Moscow 2009

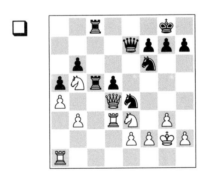

No, White can't take: this is the exception! White has three attackers of d5 versus just two defenders, but unfortunately his queen would have to 'go first' after 1.♘xd5?? ♖xd5 2.♕xd5 ♘xd5 3.♖xd5, so instead of winning a pawn, he drops his queen for only a rook and pawn.

White had a much better idea; he piled more pressure on the weak d5 pawn with 1.♖ad1!. Soon all Black's pieces were stuck defending d5 and White converted his advantage.

Power Trick #3:
Takes Takes Bang!

Here's the best way to start thinking one and a half power moves ahead. Let's say you have a chance to take a protected piece or make a trade. In some games, you may have chances like that almost every turn!

Here's what I want you to do: try looking 1.5 power moves ahead, by saying: 'If I take, he takes back, and *then* what can I do?' Answering this simple question is going to win you lots of chess games.

Really?

Sure! It works for the masters, and it will work for you too. The trick is to work on your board sight so you can visualize any winning second moves after the two captures on move one.

Stefansson-Kasparov, Reykjavik 1995

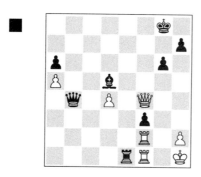

Did you use the values? Ex-World Champion Garry Kasparov is down a rook for bishop and pawn (one point). How does he think about this position?

A trade is possible, so he must start by calculating: **1...♖xf1+** (Takes) **2.♖xf1** (Takes)...
(see next page)

2...f2+ (Bang!!) This tremendous power move uncovers a check by the bishop, while also defending the white ♔'s escape square g1. Mate next! By finding a winning tactic after the trade, Garry knocked off a strong grandmaster.

Rodriguez Lopez-Vassallo Barroche, Corrado Villalba, 2008

This one looks tricky, but Black uses great *board sight* to discover that making a trade opens a winning line for his queen:

1...♗xf2! (Takes) **2.♖xf2** (Takes)

2...♕h1#! (Bang!).

Want to know why Takes Takes Bang! is such a strong trick? Because taking a piece is very **forcing**. A forcing move gives the opponent very few good options. White's recapture 2.♖xf2 above allowed checkmate, but even if White didn't take back, he'd be down a knight for nothing. In fact, in the game White tried the desperate 2.e6, but after 2...♕a6+ he resigned anyway. Also 2.♕g5+ ♔f8 wouldn't change the outcome. By using power tricks #3 and #4, you're not just *hoping* that your opponent falls into a trap: you're *forcing* him into it with 1.5 power move calculation. You replace Mr. James' 'I go here, then I go here', with thinking ahead like the pros.

Even if a trade doesn't lead to checkmate, it may win material if you can see 1.5 power moves ahead:

I. Sokolov-McShane, London 2009

White has a choice of forcing trades in this complicated middlegame, but look for the best to win the game at once! 1.♘xd7+? ♘xd7! is okay for Black, so next he calculates **1.♗xc5** (Takes – and also protects his rook and knight) **1...♕xc5** (Takes) **2.♘xd7+** (Bang!!). What a crusher! White takes a free bishop, while double attacking the ♔+♕! Black's queen falls next.

Neumann-Mayet, Berlin 1865

The dangerous dinosaur Neumann probably looked at 1.♕d5 to attack Black's ♖a8, but saw that 1...♖b8 sets up the exception to the Quick Count: White has two attackers of g8 against one defender, but he can't take because his strongest piece (the queen) has to go first: 2.♕xg8? ♖xg8.

But he solved that problem quickly with a more forcing first move:
1.♗xg8 (Takes) **1...♖xg8** (Takes) **2.♕d5** (Bang!!)

Now the white queen is attacking both rooks and one must fall, so Black resigned.

Ready for another great master secret? It's time to go one step further with Takes Takes Bang! To get the most out of it, use this trick to analyze *all captures* – not just even trades, but also positions where you sacrifice big material, including your queen.

Perez de Aranda-Ponce Lopez, Corrado Villalba 2008

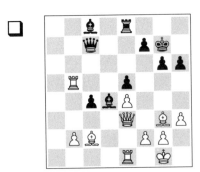

Black has just blundered a bishop, but would your board sight be able to spot it quickly? It will if you practice Takes Takes Bang! even when it means giving the queen! **1.♕xd4!** (Takes) **1...exd4** (Takes) **2.♗xc7** (Bang!!).

Oops!! It turns out that the black bishop wasn't really protected, but to see it you had to calculate 1.5 power moves ahead, an easy task here once you're in the habit of using Takes Takes Bang!

The back rank checkmate is the first mate that most people learn, so most of you have seen it.

Whether you already know this basic idea or are just learning it now, you can learn an important lesson from the great American former World Champ Bobby Fischer, who used a Takes Takes Bang! queen sacrifice to checkmate the enemy king on the back row:

Bredoff-Fischer, San Francisco 1957

Is the ♖e5 actually protected? Fischer used 1.5 power move calculation to find the answer: not really!

1...♕xe5! (Takes) **2.♖xe5** (Takes) **2...♖d1+!** (Bang!!)

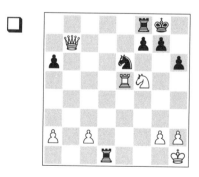

Here we have a classic back rank checkmate – the white ♔'s escape is blocked by his own pawns. White is mated after the useless interpolation 3.♖e1 ♖xe1#.

The first official World Chess Champion was the great dinosaur player Wilhelm Steinitz, often called 'the father of positional play'. He was one of the first masters to understand the importance of building up small advantages and defending well, instead of just going for the kill. But he was still deadly when he had the chance to attack.

Here he suddenly sacrifices his queen for just a knight. Was he crazy?

No, he just remembered to look out for Takes Takes Bang!

Steinitz-Gelbfuhs, Vienna 1873

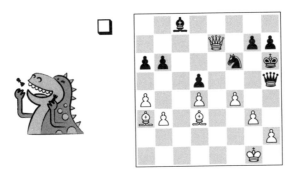

1.♕xf6+! (Takes) **1...gxf6** (Takes) **2.♗f8#** (Bang!!)

Finding this beautiful checkmate takes good board sight! You have to notice that the queen sac clears the f8-square for the bishop, and that Black's pawn capture exposes the king to a check. Finally, you have to see how all Black's escapes are covered! Still... you can find this great 1.5 move combination if you practice Takes Takes Bang! and work hard to see what's really happening on the board.

By the way, 1...♕g6 was a better try for Black, but then he's lost a knight for nothing and would have no hope against the champ.

Here's one more Takes Takes Bang! sacrifice from a rapid play game between two of the world's best players! This time Black doesn't sacrifice the queen – just a rook for a bishop. But the result is just as spectacular:

(see next page)

Topalov-Kasparov, Sofia rapid match, 1998

Now I know which move to look at first – 1...♖xf1+!.

Excellent, you're getting the hang of it! When you have the possibility of a Takes Takes Bang! exchange or sacrifice, that's the first thing you should look at. Often it wins the game, and it's easy to calculate because it's so *forcing* – the opponent usually has no good alternatives to confuse you with.

So here we go:

1...♖xf1+ (Takes) **2.♔xf1** (Takes) **2...♕h1#** (Bang!!)

Thanks Zort – that's a nice mate to look at! It's a kind of modified back-rank mate, with the (pinned!) ♘d4 and the queen preventing the white ♔ from escaping forward.

Yeah, thanks *a lot* Zort – not!! I saw that one with my own board sight!

All right then, good job – let's see if you can solve the following problems.

Takes Takes Bang! Exercises

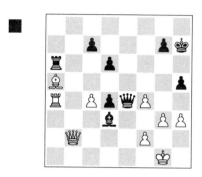

Calculate 1.5 power moves ahead to win a bishop.

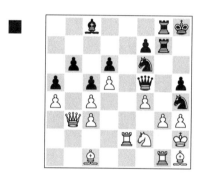

Can you find Grandmaster Nimzowitsch's fantastic Takes Takes Bang! mate?

Takes Takes Bang! Solutions

Addison-Fischer, New York 1969

1...♖xa5! (Takes) 2.♖xa5 (Takes) 2...♕e1+ (Bang!!) regains the rook with 3...♕xa5 and wins a bishop.

Johner-Nimzowitsch (variation), Dresden 1926

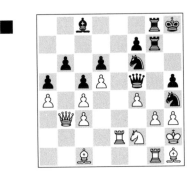

Remember to consider all Takes Takes Bang! power move possibilities, even if they look silly at first! Especially when attacking the king! Nimzowitsch planned an amazing 1.5 power move combo to break White's defenses

1...♕xh3+!! 2.♘xh3 ♘g4#!

This one takes fantastic board sight to see how both white defenders of the g4-square are removed. To become a real tiger, you have to learn to visualize the position accurately after 1.5 power moves – but you will if you keep practicing! Like learning to play a musical instrument, it takes time and concentration to do it well. Try to *visualize* Nimzowitsch's mate in your head, until you can see why White's king is history. This visualizing helps you develop powerful board sight.

Power Trick #4:
Check Moves Bang!

Here's the last power trick to help you calculate 1.5 power moves ahead. Once you understand this one, you'll be ready to learn all the best master tactics!

Remember why Takes Takes Bang! was such a great way to find winning moves?

Yes! Because captures are very forcing, they don't give the opponent many good options.

Great memory! Well, *checking* the enemy king is another good way to limit his options. So every time you have a chance to play a check, you should do the same thing you did with Takes Takes Bang!-try to see 1.5 power moves ahead.

How?

Easy: calculate your check, his options to escape, and your strongest power move on move two. Here's a common example:

Gossip-Schiffers, Breslau 1887

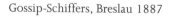

The values say White is two pawns ahead, but he resigned after **1...♛e1+** (Check) **2.♚b2** (Moves) **2...♛xd2** (Bang!!), winning the knight and soon more.

This one was fairly easy to find: Black had just one good check, and White only one legal answer! The killer queen check pried the white ♚ from the defense of his knight.

Motoc-Mijovic, Litohoro U-14 Girls, 1999

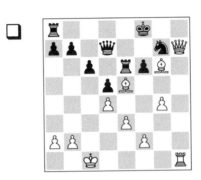

Young Alina Motoc didn't worry too much about the attack on her bishop. She remembered to look out for **power tricks** and destroyed Black's defenses with a simple queen check like last example:

1.♛h8+! (Check) **1...♚e7** (Moves) **2.♛xg7+** (Bang!!). Black resigned due to checkmate in three: 2...♚d8 3.♜h8+ ♜e8 4.♜xe8+ ♛e8 5.♛c7#. (Sorry, Zort is in sleep mode! You might want to play out the pretty checkmate yourself.)

Taimanov-Fischer, Vancouver 1971

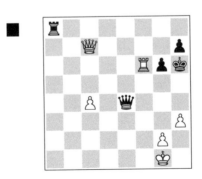

White is a pawn ahead, but he misses a simple Check Moves Bang! combination that wins the game:

1...♕d4+! (Check) attacks the king and rook, so White must try **2.♖f2** (Moves), but now comes the stinger **2...♖a1+!** (Bang!!), forcing the white ♔ to abandon his rook (the ♖f2 can't block the check because he is pinned by the black ♕).

Is the queen the only piece that starts **Check Moves Bang**?

No! She's the best at it because of her mobility, but of course any piece can start a **Check Moves Bang!** power trick:

Torres Samper-Elissalt Cardenas, Collado Villalba 2008

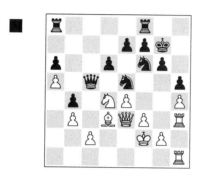

Black sees a **double attack** on White's king and queen. The key square looks protected, but it isn't really, if you can see 1.5 power moves ahead:
1...♘eg4+! (Check) **2.fxg4** (Moves) **2...♘xg4+** (Bang!)

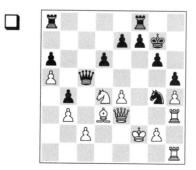

Position after 2...♘xg4+

It's a crushing **knight fork** which we'll study next chapter. Black takes the queen next move and wins easily.

Check Moves Bang! is also a great way to checkmate the enemy king.

Kasparov-Rachels, New York simul, 1988

Black has played the tricky defensive move ...♕c1?. It looks great, because he's a bishop and pawn ahead and wants to trade queens. If 1.♕xc1?? ♞xc1 the 'hook-up' trick has saved Black's knight from being taken by the ♖g3.

But the great champ was ready with **1.♞f7+!** (Check) **1...♖xf7** (Moves) **2.♕b8+** (Bang!!). With the ♖g3 blocking the black ♚'s escape, checkmate on the back row soon follows!

Mahescandra-Cochrane, Calcutta 1854

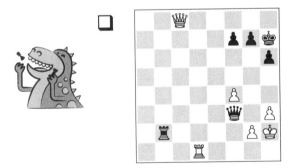

Remember this key Check Moves Bang! trick that was already well known by the early dinosaurs. Black threatens checkmate on g2, but White comes first.

1.♕f5+! (Check) **1...g6** (Moves) (or 1...♚g8 2.♖d8#) **2.♕xf7+** (Bang!!) White has stripped the black ♚'s cover with check, and it's all over now: **2...♚h8 3.♖d8#**.

Did your board sight help you notice that White's ♙g2 is pinned by the black rook and can't take the queen?

Yeah, I saw it! That finish was exciting! I kind of like those old dinosaur games.

Often the key to a winning Check Moves Bang! sequence is to find the *right* check among several good options. There are only two ways to do it!

1. Hope you get lucky, or
2. Think 1.5 power moves ahead by calculating your opponent's response, and your best second move, against each different checking possibility.

T. Hansen-Carlsen, Oslo 2006

Using the values shows White is two points up, but his king is exposed. Black has two checking options on h1 or e1. But on 1...♛h1+ 2.♔g3, there's no good 'Bang' on move two for Black (if 2...♛h3+? 3.♔f2 the king slips away, and White wins!). So he calculates the other try:

1...♛e1+! (Check) **2.♛g3** (Moves) **2...♛h1+** (Bang!!) and mate next! The *right* check forced White's queen onto the g3-square, taking away the king's only escape hatch.

Here's one more beautiful Check Moves Bang! mate by the great Kasparov:
(see next page)

Knezevic-Kasparov, Banja Luka 1979

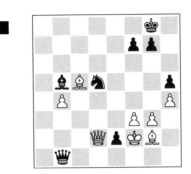

You can use a quick count to see that White has defended against 1...e1♕+??.
He has two attackers there against only one black defender, so 2.♕xe1 wins the
new queen. But Kasparov found another fantastic Check Moves Bang! option:
1...♕f1+!! (Check) **2.♗xf1** (Takes) **2...exf1♕#** (Bang!!)

Terrific board sight! Garry remembered to calculate *all* the queen checks, even
one that gave the queen. Stay alert for great surprise forcing moves when your
pawn is so close to queening.

Check Moves Bang! Exercises

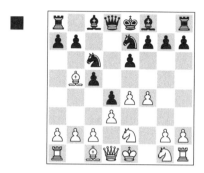

Win a Piece in 1.5 Power Moves.

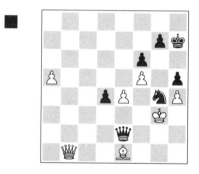

Calculate the pretty Check Moves Bang! checkmate!

Check Moves Bang! Solutions

Simons-Loewe, London 1849

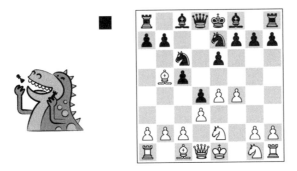

1...♕a5+! (Check) **2.♗d2** (Moves) **2...♕xb5** (Bang!) is an important elementary queen fork which we'll study a lot in the next chapter.

Mason-Mackenzie, Paris 1878

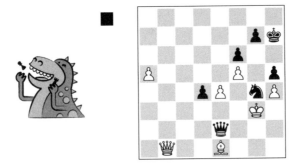

Black found the *right* check by looking 1.5 power moves ahead:
1...♕h2+! (Check) **2.♔f3** (Moves) **2...♘e5#** (Bang!!)

Cool! I can't wait to try out these power tricks on my friends!

Congratulations! Now that you've learned the four key power tricks for thinking ahead, you're ready to begin learning all the great master tactics that win games.

Chapter 2

Forks

'My piece attacks two of yours – which one do you want to lose?'

A **fork** is a move which attacks two or more enemy pieces at the same time. Since both enemy pieces can't escape at once, the forking piece usually wins one of the forked pieces next move.

Forks are the most *democratic* power move tactic. Any piece can do it, even the pawn or king! For this reason, forks are a very common master tactic. But just because we call something 'common' or 'basic' in chess, that doesn't mean it's easy to see! Even grandmasters play, and fall into forks all the time!

That's true, kids. I always look for forks in my calculations, and often find them! Try to understand the forking power of every piece. You'll win many games this way.

Pawn Forks

Anderssen-Szen (variation), London 1851

In this variation from a showdown between two famous dinosaurs, White is able to land the ultimate pawn fork **1.g4+!**, forking king and queen! Notice the key role of the supporting pawn on h3: without it, Black would just snap off the g-pawn and win, but now Black loses the lady for just two pawns after 1...♕xg4 2.hxg4+ ♔xg4.

While lots of kids in your school could fall right into such a killer fork, you have to trick a stronger player into it by seeing ahead with power move calculation:

Anderssen-Kieseritzky, London 1851

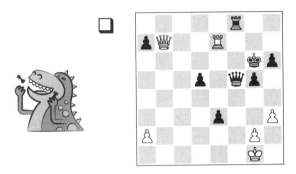

Black has two beautiful passed pawns, but White's well-calculated 1.5 power moves show that the black ♚ is too exposed:

1.♖g7+ ♚h5 Now you know what to do. But to become a tactical tiger, you have to be ready with a strong answer even if he doesn't fall for the fork! On 1...♚f6 White had an even stronger move: 2.♕e7#!
2.g4+ 1-0

Hey, that's the same pawn fork as in the first example!

Right! Recognizing the *pattern* makes power move calculation much easier.

Yoffie-Diatsintos, Haifa 1970

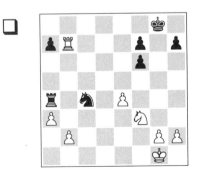

When a pawn forks rooks or knights, it doesn't even *need* support, since those two pieces can't move diagonally to take it.

1.b3! ♖xa3

But when you play a power tactic, your opponent is going to try to slip out of it! White saw the counterattack 2...♘d6 2.♖b8+! when the check lets his rook slip away, and he captures Black's rook next move.

2.bxc4 gets a free knight, a winning edge for a master.

Many forks and other tactics use the Takes Takes Bang! power trick we learned in Chapter One. To find them you just have to see 1.5 power moves ahead, starting with a capture:

Bird-Medley, London 1849

The black ♗ can take two different pieces:

1...♗xe3+! (Takes) **2.♕xe3** (Takes) **2...d4!** (Bang!! – a winning pawn fork!) White has no tricks this time, so he resigns.

By the way, the other piece capture also won: 1...♗xc3 2.bxc3 d4 with a discovered attack, which we will see more of in *Power Chess: Book 2*.

Zaichik-Sikharulidze, USSR 1976

In this cool example, a pawn fork forces Black's bishop into a queen fork.

1.e4!

A great example of a master power move! It looks losing because Black can take the unsupported pawn, but White has calculated a winning tactical response:

1...♗xe4 2.♕a4+!

The point – the pawn fork set up a winning Check Moves Bang! queen fork. 3.♕xe4 next grabs a bishop.

When your pawn moves to the 7th rank and forks two enemy pieces, it's ready to become a new queen. This gives rise to some tremendous power moves.

Sznapik-Bernard, Poznan 1971

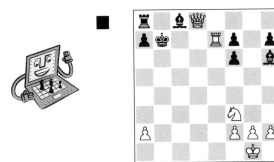

The values show White is a piece down in the ending, but he's calculated a beautiful winning move that sets up a power pawn fork:

1.♖d8!! This is power chess! Most players would never even think of a move that seems to lose a rook for nothing. But to figure out that it wins, you only have to use great board sight and think 1.5 power moves ahead.

1...♖xd8

He must take because of the neat hidden mate threat 1...♗g7 2.♖b7#!: the pinned c8 bishop can't take the rook.

2.c7+ Killer fork!! **2...♔b7 3.cxd8♕+**

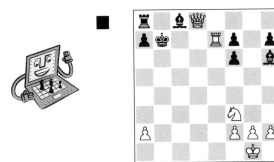

White not only makes a queen, but discovers check with the rook. Black is dead.

See kids, Mr. Hertan is right! If you can see amazing power moves like that, one and a half moves ahead, you'll be the strongest kid around!

Duh! No kidding, professor! That one was *really* awesome.

Here's one more position where Black used a power pawn fork to make a new queen. This time Bobby Fischer lost to another former World Champ, the elegant positional maestro Vassily Smyslov.

Fischer-Smyslov, Bled/Zagreb/Belgrade 1959

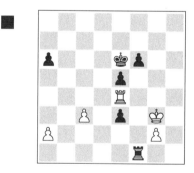

The forcing move **1...f5!** won on the spot. **2.♖xe3 f4+** is a deadly pawn fork, while on other rook moves 2...e2 makes a new queen.

Knight Forks

The tricky knight is one of the most famous and effective forkers. His weird 'L-shaped' move, and unique power of jumping over other pieces, make the ♘ very good at surprise attacks. Recognizing knight forks will help you win many games, and avoid as many traps.

Schrems-Korsus, Bad Wiessee 2008

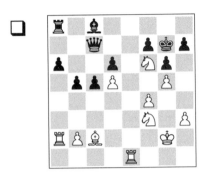

Did you remember to count the values first? White is already even with a rook and two knights against queen and two pawns, so Black can forget about it after **1.♘e8+!**, a so-called **royal fork**. Royal forks attack ♚ and ♛, winning the lady for free!

The knight casts a kind of spider's web around the board, when he's in the middle and controls 8 different squares! In this position two pieces on opposite sides of the board got caught in the spider's trap:

Morawietz-J. Grant, Bad Wiessee 2008

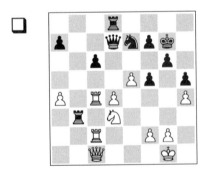

1.♘c5! 1-0
The naughty knight even stops 1...♛b7 so Black must lose a whole rook.

Three great knight forking squares: c7, e7, and f7

From the starting position your knights can hop to these three squares in 3 moves! Often your opponent's pawns can chase the knight before he does any damage, but if not, you might get to play a killer knight fork!

Power Knight Fork #1:
♘c7 (or c2 for Black)

Canal-Colle, Karlsbad 1929

Black forks White's rooks in 1.5 power moves to win rook for knight after **1...♘b4! 2.♕f3 ♘c2**.

S. Short-Ahern, Cork 2005

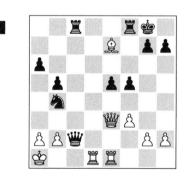

If the ♘ could get to c2 he could land a royal fork, so:
1...♕xd1+! (Takes) **2.♖xd1** (Takes) **2...♘c2+** (Bang!)
Black wins a whole rook after 3.♔b1 ♘xe3 4.♖e1 ♘xg2 5.♖g1 ♖fe8. He remembered to calculate all captures 1.5 power moves ahead, even one that gave the queen.

Power Knight Fork #2:
♘f7 (f2 for Black)

Marshall-Capablanca (modified), New York 1927

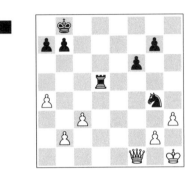

Here's a pretty f2 fork trick with the knight which has won countless games:
1...♖d1!
The white ♕ is enticed onto a forking square. In *Power Chess: Book Two* we'll look at many more 'enticement combinations'.
2.♕xd1 ♘f2+ winning the ♕ and the game.

Here's another typical f2 fork I dreamed up:

Zort (Zugzwang, 2011)

A Check Moves Bang! combination wins the queen or mates in 1.5 power moves: **1....♗d4+!** (Check) **2.♔h1** (Moves) 2.♔f1 allows the royal fork 2...♘e3+; but even stronger is 2...♘xh2 mate! **2...♘f2+** (Bang!!) spears the queen.

50

Power Knight Fork #3:

♘e7

Firman-Areschenko, Germany Bundesliga 2008

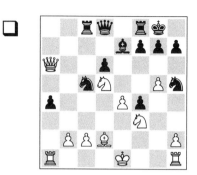

A strong grandmaster attacked White's queen with ...♘c5?? but forgot to check the 1.5 power move idea **1.♕xc8!** (Takes) **1...♕xc8** (Takes) **2.♘xe7+** (Bang!!). The fork trick recovers the queen and wins a whole rook.

Hradsky-Frisk, Olomouc 2008

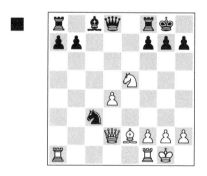

Black has a strong trade with 1...♘xe2+, but he finds a much better forcing move:

1...♕xd4!

White loses his ♘ or ♗ after this surprise power move.

2.♕xd4

The ♘ and ♕ were attacked, and if 2.♘f3 ♕xd2 3.♘xd2 ♘xe2+.

2...♘xe2+

The e2 power fork recovers the ♕ with interest.

3.♔h1 ♘xd4 and wins.

A fine **Takes Takes Bang!** combination, eh?

Family Forks

This is a fun term for a knight fork that attacks practically everything in sight:

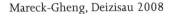

Mareck-Gheng, Deizisau 2008

Winning a rook for a knight or bishop is called 'winning the exchange'. Between strong players this two-point advantage is usually enough to win the game, unless the opponent gets a strong attack or some other big advantage in return (called 'compensation').

After **1...♘h5!** Black prepared the family fork 2...♘f4! attacking the queen and both rooks! Only one white piece could get out of the way, so he had to lose the exchange for nothing. If 2.g3 ♘xg3+ is another winning fork.

Schallop-W. Paulsen, Leipzig 1877

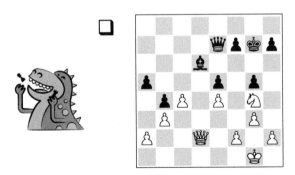

Sometimes 'backward' moves make winning attacks! After **1.♘e3!** the family fork threat on f5 wins at least a bishop: **1...♔g6 2.♘f5**.

Good board sight means looking at retreats, too.

Awesome! You never know which move could turn out to be a power move, do you?

Right! You don't know until you calculate ahead.

Let's round out our study of knight forks by looking at a few more common fork tricks. These are Takes Takes Bang! positions where you sacrifice material, but look 1.5 power moves ahead to land a winning fork.

Ruy Lopez-Leonardo, Madrid 1575

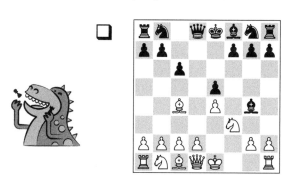

Here's a very common opening fork trick you must know:
1.♗xf7+! (Takes) **1...♔xf7** (Takes) **2.♘xe5+** (Bang!!), recovering the bishop with a two-pawn edge.

Becerra Rivero-Robson, St. Louis 2009

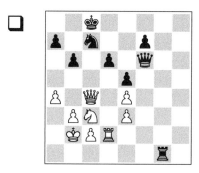

The fork trick **1.♕xc7+!** ♔xc7 **2.♘d5+** recovers the queen and wins a knight.

Bishop Forks

Hertneck-Kasparov, Munich blitz 1994

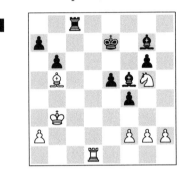

The angling bishop is a good forker too! The ex-world champ caught a grandmaster in an obviously winning bishop fork in this blitz game, with the help of his rook's protection: **1...♗c2+ 0-1**

The bishop is a 'long-range' piece, meaning it can travel from one corner to the other in just a move. Here it forks two pieces on opposite ends of the board.

Lengyel-Konnyu, Budapest 2008

1...♘xg4 (Takes) **2.fxg4** (Takes) **2...♗d4+** (Bang!), bagging the stray ♘a7. Have you noticed that the 'Bang' in a Takes Takes Bang! combo is often a strong check on move two? Remember, they're very forcing, so analyze checks and captures *first*.

Most experts think Garry Kasparov is the strongest chess player that ever lived.

I agree! Kasparov was Rad!

You mean the strongest *human* player!

OK Zort, you're right. Kasparov's tactical vision was so strong, even the best grandmasters couldn't foresee his amazing power moves in time!

Roar!!!

Sorry, lizard-face. Some people think that the great dinosaur champ Paul Morphy could have been the best ever, but he only competed for a few years! Kasparov ruled the chess world for nearly 25 years!

Here Garry sets up a *royal bishop fork*, and with power move calculation avoids a devilish trap at the same time!

Fedoruk-Kasparov, Daugavpils 1978

Once you notice that White's bishop is pinned to the queen, it becomes very tempting to play 1...♗xd4+?? 2.♗xd4 ♖xd2, winning the queen but losing the game!! Zort?

Here's a riddle, earth children, before I show the trap: what's more important than winning the queen??

Analysis position after 2...♖xd2

3.♖a8+ ♔h7 4.♖h8#!

Final analysis position after 4.♖h8#!

This is master calculation! Garry didn't just think 'I win the queen' and fall for the trap – he looked further to see if White had any good forcing moves – and White's only checks led to mate! Now let's see how Black landed a winning blow instead:

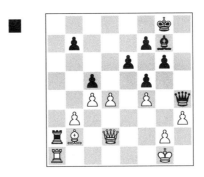

1...♖xb2! Garry finds a safe way to go after the queen. White resigned because his rook check now leads nowhere, and on 2.♕xb2 ♗xd4+ the royal bishop fork spears the ♕.

I told you Kasparov was totally *awesome*!

Lushenkov-Olenin, Sochi 2009

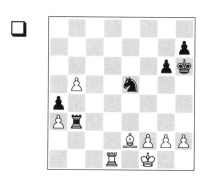

Most kids fall right into forks, but even strong adults can be tricked into them with 1.5 power move calculation. White finished with a forcing move and a ♗ fork:
1.f4! ♘f7
Did you use your board sight to see that the ♘ has no other safe squares?
2.♗c4! The bishop fork wins at least the exchange, so Black gave up.

Bishops can also play the fork trick, giving up material to get back more with a power fork. Here are some typical examples from the dinosaurs:

Rosenthal-Chigorin, London 1883

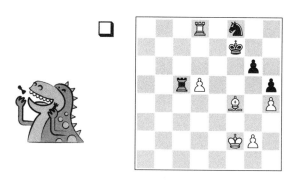

This one is tricky! The fork 1.♗d6 looks good, since after 1...♖c2+ and 2...♘h7 White can pin Black down with 3.♖d7+ en 4.♗e5. However, White finds a more forcing power move which achieves the fork trick by giving Black's rook no time to get away:

1.♖xf8!+ ♔xf8 2.♗d6+ 1-0

That wasn't so tricky – just a Takes Takes Bang! combination!

Great point! 1.♖xf8+ was the first forcing move you should analyze.

Here's a real master fork trick! The great Russian attacker Alexei Shirov saw two and a half moves ahead to score the winning tactic. Zort, come back online please!

OK Mr. Hertan, I like the games of GM Shirov!

Shirov-Vorobiov, Sochi 2009

1.♗e6!
A winning power move. The rook must defend the ♗c2.
1...♖c7

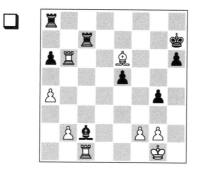

2.♖xc2!
The point. White wins a piece with a fork trick.
2...♖xc2 3.♗f5+ 1-0

 Super radical! I bet I could find that one if I practice *a lot*.

Rook Forks

E. Cardenas-Blanco Sanchez, Corrado Villalba 2008

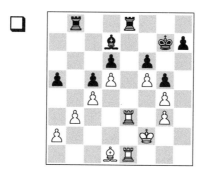

Naturally, the powerful rook is a great forker. Rook forks on the 7th row are especially common, since there are often many enemy pawns and pieces to gobble up there. Here White's strong doubled rooks on the open e-file allowed **1.♖e7+!**, winning the bishop.

Mackenzie-Rosenthal, London 1883

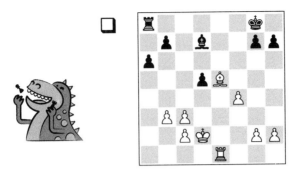

The strong Scottish dinosaur Mackenzie used a simple fork trick on the 7th row to win a decisive second pawn:

1.♗xg7! (Takes) And if Black had played **1...♔xg7** (Takes) there would have followed **2.♖e7+** (Bang!) and **3.♖xd7**.

Cochrane-Staunton, London 1842

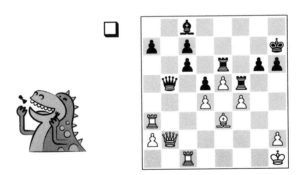

The rook's great mobility makes it the second strongest piece. Here he shows off his ability to attack horizontally (on the 'rank') and vertically (on the 'file') at the same time! It starts with another Takes Takes Bang! combination: **1.♕xb5! cxb5 2.♖xc7+**, seizing the bishop with a power fork.

The eighth row is the other rank where lots of enemy pieces are forked by a penetrating rook.

We've seen how power move tricks can lead to back rank mate, but don't forget to look out for back rank *forks* too.

Gunina-Severiukhina, Serpukhov 2008

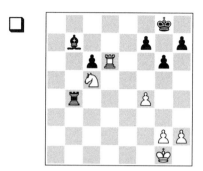

1.♖d7! won the bishop, because retreats allow the back rank fork **2.♖d8+**.

Here Black wins a piece with a Takes Takes Bang! combo forcing a rook fork:

Vaisser-Nielsen, Internet ACP Blitz, 2004

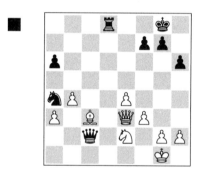

1...♘xc3! (Takes) **2.♘xc3** (Takes) If 3.♕xc3 ♕xe2. **2...♖d3!** (Bang!) **0-1**

Nimzowitsch-Menchik, Karlsbad 1929

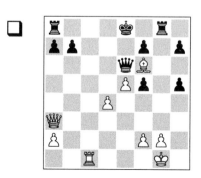

By material count (the values), you may think Black is winning here! She's ahead by three whole points, an exchange and a pawn. But material isn't everything in chess, and this position is a perfect example!

Black can't castle, so her king is exposed to attack in the middle, and her rooks are disconnected and weak. More importantly, look at White's beautiful pieces, all poised for attack! The ♗f6 is just tremendous, anchored near Black's king by the ♙e5. In this special position, he is much stronger than either black rook!!

Would you believe that Black resigned after just one more move?
1.♖c7! threatens the tremendous rook fork 2.♖e7+, when Black can't even capture due to 3.♕xe7#. Black is helpless.

Queen Forks

Every kid knows that the queen is the most powerful attacker by far! She's also the strongest forker. Like an eagle pouncing on its prey, the lady swoops down to attack several pieces on far ends of the board!

Here are some typical queen forks to spring on unwary opponents!

De Vere-Rousseau, Paris 1867

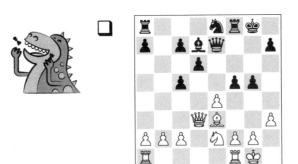

Any time you have a possible queen check, look out for a fork like this:
1.♕d5+ (Check) **2...♗e6** (Moves) **2.♕xa8** (Bang!)

One of the shortest master games ever involves a similar central queen check, forking king and rook on move five! Amazingly, it was repeated again in 2008:

I. Mayer-Heyl, Budapest 2008
1.e4 c5 2.b4 cxb4 3.a3 d5 4.exd5 ♕xd5 5.axb4??

5...♛e5+! 0-1

Von Heydebrand und der Lasa-Von Bilguer, Berlin 1837

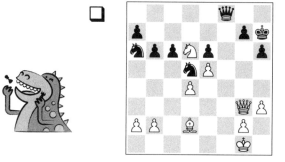

Another central queen check picks off a loose knight far across the board: **1.♕d3+! 1-0**

Stanley-Rousseau, New Orleans 1845

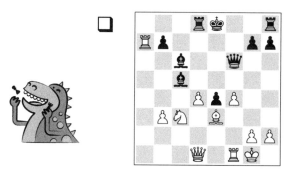

The king can also be caught in a queen fork before castling. Black was relying on the pinned d-pawn to save his bishop (1.dxc5?? ♖xd1), but he forgot something important: the queen check **1.♕h5+** (Check) **1...g6** (Moves) **2.♕xc5** (Bang!).

Don't forget to analyze the forcing check first!!

The nimble queen has plenty of mobility even from her starting square d1 (or d8 for Black)! Winning queen checks in the early opening are not unusual.

Here's another trap where many players have lost a knight on move four!
1.e4 c5 2.d4 cxd4 3.♘f3 e5

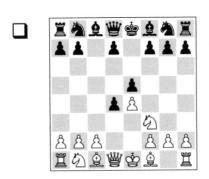

Now White should play the pawn sacrifice 4.c3! with a good game. But if he takes the bait with **4.♘xe5??** he is already lost after the forking check **4....♕a5+!**

Here are two common queen forks on the important a7-g1 diagonal (a2-g8 for White), along which the castled king is frequently attacked:

Jaenig-Llaneza Vega, Bad Wiessee 2008

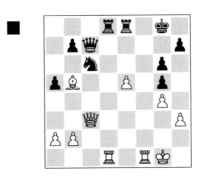

1...♕b6+! snaring the white bishop.

I used a fork trick on this key diagonal to win a key pawn against a strong master:

Dehmelt-Hertan, New York Open 1984

The 1.5 move combination **1...♗xg5!** took the wind out of White's attack and won pretty easily, because on **2.♗xg5** the fork trick **2...♕c5+!** and **3...♕xg5** regains the bishop with a healthy extra pawn, and no worries.

The winning idea was easy to miss, because in the diagram White's ♗e3 guards the a7-g1 diagonal, but my decoy power move pulled him away.

The rook isn't the only piece that likes to deliver back rank forks. The queen can do it even better with her added diagonal powers.

Ji Dan-Zhou Weiqi, Xinghua Jiangsu 2010

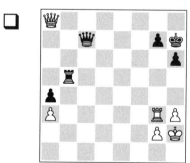

If you had white, could you find the Check Moves Bang! sequence that wins a rook? I bet you could, with a bit of work and board sight: **1.♕e4+! ♔h8** 1...♔g8 turns out the same, while 1...g6 2.♕xg6+ is mate next. **2.♕e8+!** is a back rank fork of ♔+♖.

Please notice – 1.♕xa4 was tempting, but White remembered Check Move Bang! and found a much, much better move.

Stabolewski-I. Farago, Budapest 2008

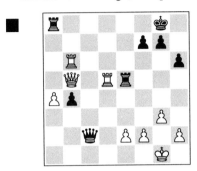

Even if no back rank forks are possible, a back rank queen *check* often leads to a fork somewhere else! Black has two safe queen checks here, but must calculate 1.5 power moves ahead to find the right one:

1...♛b1+! (Best check!) **2.♔g2** (Moves) **2...♛e4+!** (Bang!) Forking ♔+♖.

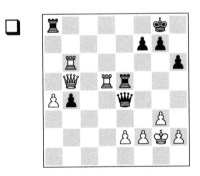

Position after 2...♛e4+!

There are almost as many queen forks as there are stars in the sky, so we will look at just one more for now.

Yudasin-Kasparov, Frunze 1981

Here's a very important type of fork we haven't discussed yet.
Black's **1...♛a5!** not only threatens the pawn on a2 and the bishop way over on h5; it also threatens checkmate in 1.5 power moves! If 2.♛h4 to defend the bishop, 2...♛xa2+ 3.♚c1 ♛a1 mates, so White resigned.

King Forks

Remember I said that forks are the most democratic power tactic? Because the ♚ plods around one square at a time, and has to always mind his royal safety, it's pretty unusual for him to get involved in power moves. When he does, it's usually a king fork later in the game, when he's no longer afraid of getting mated and feels ready to attack!

 When I googled king forks, I read they were very rare!

 Googling is my favorite hobby, but don't believe everything you read on the Web.

Fischer-Kramer, New York blitz, 1971

A king in the endgame is like an octopus in his cave. If you keep your distance he won't hurt you, but if you get too close he might jump out and bite!

1.♚g2! The octopus strikes. The best Black can do is lose the exchange with 1...♝f4 2.♚xh3 ♝xe3, but the ending is lost so he threw in the towel.

What means this 'threw in the towel'? Isn't that object used for bathing?

No, silly! It means he gave up, resigned.

Short-Kasparov, London rapid match, 1987

Garry wants to fight on with 1.axb3 a2! making a queen, but the strong Englishman Nigel Short induced resignation instead with the king fork **1.♔c2!**. (By the way, also crushing was 1.♖ef8! threatening 2.♖1f7#)

Kasparov threw in the towel?

Yes, you silly silicon simpleton!

What's a simpleton?

A dummy, an idiot!

Hey, I resemble that remark! I mean resent! Computer malfunction. Unknown error. Please restart.

Wallenrath-Von Jaenisch, St. Petersburg 1850

1.♔f3! was the strongest possible ♔ fork (kings can't attack queens, only capture them if they come too close!). White overcame a few more tricks to win.

We haven't talked about this yet, but when someone springs a tactic on you, you can try using power moves to get out of it, by calculating a little further ahead! The ex-champ allowed a strong-looking king fork here, finding a stronger 1.5 power move answer.

P. Nikolic-Kasparov, Wijk aan Zee 2000

The king fork **1.♔d4** was met by **1...♗b3!**.

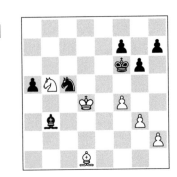

Position after 1...♗b3!

I call this a 'hook-up' combination because the connection of Black's pieces allows both to escape on 2.♗xb3 ♘xb3+, while on 2.♔xc5 the counter threat 2...♗xd1 saves the day. Never give up when you fall for a tactic – look for a way out like Garry's 1...♗b3!.

And when you're about to play a tactic, take one more look around to make sure it doesn't have any obvious loopholes – like mate or loss of your queen!

Forks: Exercises

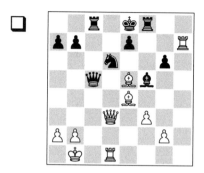

Find a Takes Takes Bang! sacrifice to land a crushing ♗ fork.

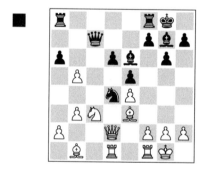

Sacrifice big for a winning ♘ fork trick.

Forks: Solutions

Eastwood-Baumber, Sunderland 1966

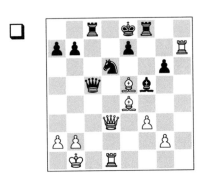

The most forcing move, **1.♖xe7+! ♔xe7 2.♗xd6+**, is devastation. But not the lazy 1.♗xd6 exd6 2.♕xd6?? ♗xe4+ 4.fxe4 ♕c2+, mating for Black!

Pert-Ward, Douglas 2005

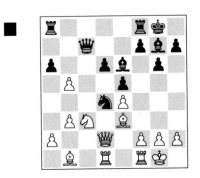

White has overlooked a 1.5 power move shot on the key e2 forking square: **1...♕xc3!** (Takes) **2.♕xc3** (Takes) **2...♘e2+** (Bang!) regaining the ♕ to come out a knight ahead.

Forks: Exercises

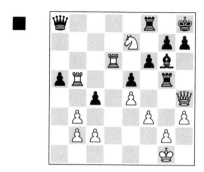

Scoop up the ♘ with a long ♛ fork.

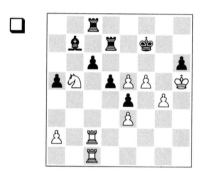

Find the strongest fork.

Forks: Solutions

Fichtinger-Scharler, Vienna 2008

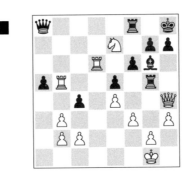

Oops! With a distant forking check on the key a7-g1 diagonal, **1...♕a7+!**, the ♘e7 is a goner. A Check Moves Bang! combo using good long-range board sight.

Menchik-Becker, Karlsbad 1929

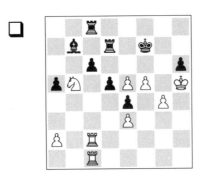

Even better than the knight fork 1.♘d6+ was the killer pawn fork **1.e6+ 1-0!**

Forks: Exercises

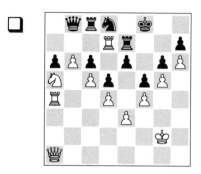

Set up a winning 'family fork'.

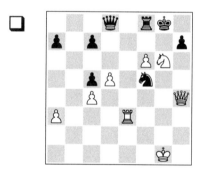

Use fantastic power move calculation to force a pawn fork.

Forks: Solutions

Capablanca-Treybal, Karlsbad 1929

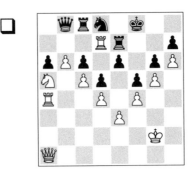

José Raoul Capablanca, the great Cuban World Champion of the 1920's, broke Black's defenses with **1.♖xd8+! ♖xd8 2.♘xc6.** White regains the exchange and scoops the a6 pawn too, with an easy win.

Sämisch-Grünfeld, Karlsbad 1929

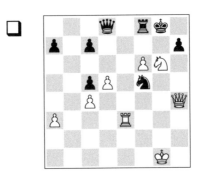

We're giving Zort an end-of-chapter rest, so please play out this pretty one yourself:

1.♖e7!! was a very beautiful win, but take full credit for the simpler 1.♘e7+ winning a ♘ since 1...♘xe7 2.fxe7 is a crushing pawn fork. **1...♖f7** Taking the ♕ allows 1...♘xh4 2.♖g7#! while 1...♘xe7 2.fxe7 is the same killer pawn fork. **2.♖xf7! ♚xf7** He still can't take the queen due to mate on g7. **3.♘e5+ ♚f8 4.♕xh7.** Black finally gives up because 5.♕h8# or 5.♕xf5 are threatened, and on 4...♕xf6 comes the 'royal ♘ fork' 5.♘d7+!

Chapter 3

Pins

'You better stay where you are, enemy piece, or I'll take your stronger friend!'

The second great master tactic is the pin. Pins are one of the most important ideas in chess! They win games all the time, in lots of different ways! Only three different pieces can make pins: the *bishop, rook, and queen*.

Why? That's not fair!

Because pins use the power of pieces along a *line of squares*, and only those three can move on a line. The *basic idea* of a pin is this:

You attack a piece with your bishop, rook, or queen, and that piece is unable to move away without material loss, because if it does move, another piece behind it will be taken.

Absolute pins

When a piece is pinned to your ♔, it can't move off the king's line, because exposing your ♔ to direct capture is an illegal move. There's a special name for these pins targeting the king: **absolute pins**. Absolute pins are super dangerous: pieces pinned to the king are often lost – and then the king may also be endangered!

Danielian-Miroshnichenko, Cappelle la Grande 2009

Here's the strongest bishop pin: an absolute pin of the queen!

1...♗d4!

Like being caught by zombies in a horror movie, the white ♕ is glued to the ♔'s defense and paralyzed!

2.♕xd4+

♗ for ♕ is all White can get; a lousy bargain!

2...cxd4 3.c7 ♘e7!

Black stops the queening threat and White can safely resign.

Semprun Martinez-Pozo Vera, Collado Villalba 2008

Look closely at this position. White's ♔+♕ are on the same diagonal. If only Black's ♗ could reach c6, he could make a royal pin. But winning depends on power move calculation! 1...♘xe5+?? doesn't work due to 2.fxe5 ♗c6 3.♕xc6! and *White* wins because of the absolute pin on the b7 pawn by the ♖b1! So, does Black forget the pinning idea? No, he finds the right way to threaten 2...♗c6:

 1...♘a5! (1...♘d8! also works) What a move! It stops 2.♕xb7#, threatens 2...♗c6 3.♕xc6 ♘xc6, and mates if White tries to avoid the pin: 2.♕g6 ♗c6+ 3.♔e2 ♕e1#. White 'threw in the towel'!

Zhao Xue-Zhang Xiaowen, Xinghua Jiangsu 2009

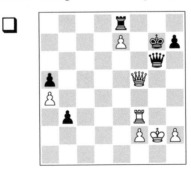

1.♖g3! pins queen to king, winning her for a rook.
If **1...♖xe7 2.♖xg6+ hxg6**, simplest is **3.♕b5**, corralling the passed b-pawn, with an easy win.

The most common absolute rook pins are on the 8th and 7th rank, where the enemy king usually hides:

McShane-Shengelia, Novi Sad 2009

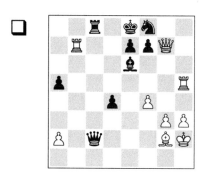

1.♖h8! is a crushing absolute pin. Black can threaten mate with the pin 1...♗d5, but 2.♖xf8# comes first.

Chapman-Kortchnoi, London 2009

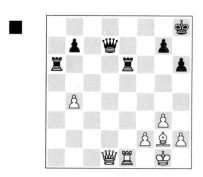

2.5 power move calculation forced an absolute pin on the back rank:
1...♖ad6! 2.♕c1 sets up a Takes Takes Bang! shot: **2...♖xe1+ 3.♕xe1 ♖d1** winning the ♕.

Once you're really good at seeing 1.5 power move combos, seeing an extra move ahead like this is the next step!

Bjerring-Hvenekilde, Copenhagen 1987

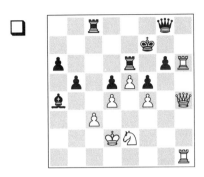

A Check Moves Bang! combination forces the king into position for a back-rank pin: **1.♖h7+! ♚e8 2.♖h8** pins and wins the queen.

Nakamura-Shulman (variation), St. Louis 2010

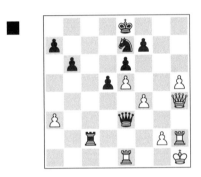

Here's an extremely important back rank rook pin to remember. A material count shows that White is up the exchange, or two points. If it were his move, White would win with 1.♖h3.

But Black had the whole position planned out with the winning pin **1...♖c1!**. Instead of moving the queen, Black pins and wins the white rook, since on 2.♖xc1 ♛xc1+ ends in back rank mate! White saw it coming and resigned a move earlier.

Whoa! Next time I'll think twice before defending my queen so fast!

Absolute Pins: Exercises

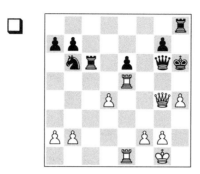

Use a Quick Count to pin the black ♛.

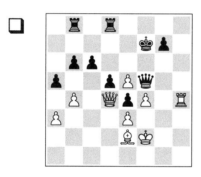

Win another queen with a 1.5 power move absolute pin.

Absolute Pins: Solutions

Tkachiev-Svidler, Almaty Wch Blitz, 2008

A quick count shows three vs. two attackers on e6, and the second white capture makes a royal pin:
1.♖xe6 ♖xe6 2.♖xe6 bags the lady.

Bogoljubow-Menchik, Karlsbad 1929

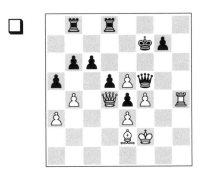

You know that captures and checks are very forcing. Well, attacking the enemy queen also limits the opponent's options, and if you can see 1.5 power moves ahead, it may win!
1.♗g4! left the black ♛ high and dry, because **1...♛g6 2.♗h5!** pins and wins her.

Cool! I'll call it a '**Queen Attack Moves Bang!**' combination!

Relative Pins

With **relative pins**, a piece is pinned to another, stronger piece, but not the king. This gives the opponent more chance to slip out of the pin, but if he can't, a relative pin may be just as winning as an absolute one:

Carlsen-Yakovich, Moscow 2004

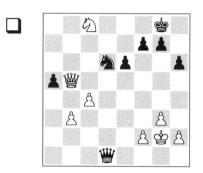

Magnus Carlsen may be the strongest teenage chess player ever!! Early in 2010 he became the top-rated player in the world, at age 19! Most chess experts believe that he will soon become World Champion. Here he found a winning relative pin:

1.♕d7! pins knight to the queen. Black resigned since the ♘ is lost.

Ruck-Neubauer, Austria 2008/09

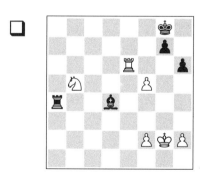

1.♖e4! froze and won Black's bishop by pinning it to the rook:
1...♖b4 2.♘xd4 1-0

Volokitin-Vorobiov, Sochi 2009

White quite correctly pins the black bishop with **1.♕b2!**, exploiting Black's uncoordinated army. Surprisingly, there is no good defense to 2.♖xb5. If 1...exd4, simplest is 2.♘xd4 adding a third attacker against b5. Black is lost.

But my teacher said never put your queen on the same file as the enemy rook!

That is wise advice, but he forgot to teach you an even more important rule: **never say never** in chess or life! Here's something really cool about chess: an idea may be wrong *almost* always, and still be the *only* good move in a particular situation.

General rules are great, but power move calculation tells you when to go against them. 1.♕b2! was clearly the best move on the board here, because 1.5 power move calculation showed it won the ♗ using the b-file pin.

Relative Pins: Exercises

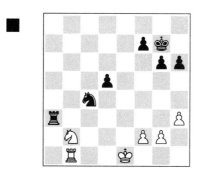

Pin and win a piece.

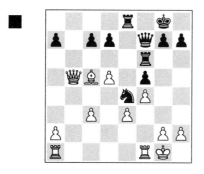

Show how a simple relative pin made White resign.

Relative Pins: Solutions

La Rota-Stripunsky, Boca Raton 2008

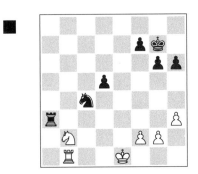

1...♖b3! pinned and won White's knight on the b-file.

Matisons-Canal, Karlsbad 1929

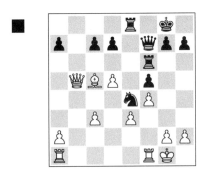

The obvious shot **1...♕xd5!** pins the white ♗ to the queen and kills it next move.

Power Moves to Exploit Pins

Want to know a secret about why pins are the most dangerous power move tactic?

You better tell me right now! I hate secrets.

OK then. Most master tactics only work for one move. If you miss your chance for a winning fork, he can probably prevent it next turn. But pins often last a long time, and can be very difficult for him to 'break'! In these cases, we say that the pin puts *pressure* on the enemy position.

Even when a pin doesn't seem to win immediately, two types of power moves can often be used to convert pins into material gain or mate. The first is the **pile-up**, and the second is the **sneaky pin**. Either of these winning ideas can be used with both relative and absolute pins, but the sneaky pin is extra good at catching the enemy king off guard!

Pin-Exploiting Moves #1:

The Pile-up Pin

Fischer-Gheorghiu, Buenos Aires 1970

When a pin can't be safely broken, the winning strategy is often to pile up on the pinned piece, preferably with the cheapest unit possible. In this case that meant **1.f3!**. Because the knight is absolutely pinned, the lowly pawn will take it next move, so Black resigned.

Barnes-Mongredien, London 1862

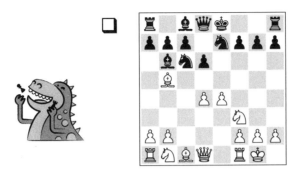

Here is a very common diagonal pile-up pin in the opening. The ♗b5 creates an absolute pin against the ♘c6, so of course White looks to pile up on it with his cheapest man:

1.d5!

Other moves miss White's chance; 8.♘c3? 0-0, escaping the pin with no damage. Power moves require alertness!

1...a6

Hoping for the trade 9.dxc6? axb5.

2.♗a4!

Maintaining the pin: 3.dxc6 next move wins the knight for a pawn.

Matlakov-Ulko, Sochi 2009

Here White piles up with two extra attackers at once!

1.♖d4! attacks the paralyzed black ♘ with the ♖, and also uncovers an extra attack by the ♕! A Quick Count shows 3 white attackers against 2 defenders, and Black can't reinforce it, so the pinned knight falls.

The ♕ fork 1.♕g4! was also winning; if 1...f5? 2.♕xg6+.

Wyvill-Anderssen, London 1851

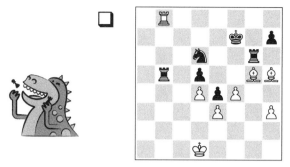

The values tell you Black is a point ahead, but the pinned ♖g6 means White can regain the exchange. But 1.♗xg6+? cashes in on the pin too soon. Instead of giving a bishop to get the rook, White can use a Takes Takes Bang! combination to pile up with a cheaper unit, and win the rook for only a pawn.

1.♖xb5!

Black's knight is overworked, a power tactic we will study more in Book 2.

1...♘xb5 2.f5! 1-0

Mitzka-Reder, Vienna 2008

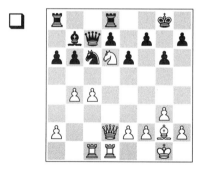

Takes Takes Bang! creates a winning diagonal pile-up.

1.♘xb7! ♕xb7 First, the black queen is forced onto the ♗g2's line, so now the ♘c6 is pinned, and... **2.b5!** (Bang!). Second, White piles up with his cheapest piece and wins the pinned knight after 2...axb5 3.cxb5. A great 1-2 punch!

Charles Hertan, on my planet it's against tournament rules to punch the opponent.

You better rest your memory before I punch you!

Popert-Staunton, London 1841

White finds a sneaky way to reinforce the absolute pin on the diagonal. **1.♗b3!** Did you use the values to count that White is up an exchange in the diagram? Using power move calculation, even after the dangerous check **1...♘f2+! 2.♖xf2! ♗xf2** White increases his advantage to a whole knight plus attack after **3.♘d6!**, which is even stronger than the immediate 3.♕xe6+.

'Vertical' pile-ups

Rooks love open files, where they have more room to operate and can often invade the enemy camp. Probably the most common pile-up pins occur when your active rook pins an enemy piece on the file. Sometimes just putting your rook where he belongs sets up a winning pin:

Thomsen-Kasparov, Torshavn simul, 2001

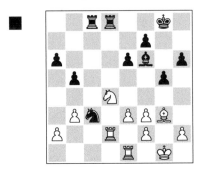

Black's rooks are positioned perfectly on the two open files. Putting your pieces on good squares often sets up power moves! The Quick Count shows White's knight is currently defended, but the pile-up **1...e5!** wins it for a pawn, since the retreats that could defend his rook, f3 and b3, are blocked by White's own pawns.

We spoke earlier about the dangers of leaving your queen on the same open file as an enemy rook. If you get your opponent in this situation, try to exploit it with a pile-up pin:

Parnell-Barry, Dublin 1865

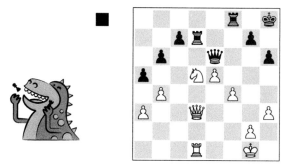

1...c6! is a simple winning pile-up because White's queen is in harm's way. Counterattacking with 2.f5 ♖xf5 3.♘f4 only makes matters worse: 3...♖xd3 4.♘xe6 ♖xd1+.

The other pile-up 1...♖fd8! also wins, once you correctly calculate the power moves.

Here's a typical vertical pile-up pin by the queen:

M. Szabo-O. Dobos, Budapest 2008

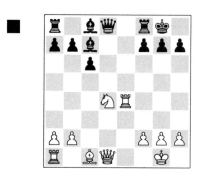

1...c5! paralyzed and won the pinned knight.

If you can't pile up on the pinned piece with a pawn, your other pieces may still do the job: (see next page)

Blackburne-Puller, London 1862

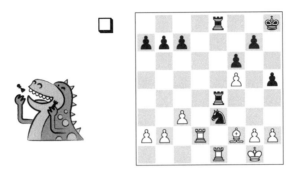

1.罝de2! won the knight. Doubling rooks on a file like this is a great way to pile up and increase pressure. But if Black's 罝e4 were on e5 instead, he could slip out with 1...②xf5!.

Great teamwork! Every white piece ganged up on the poor pinned knight.

Pawn breaks and pile-ups

Pawn breaks are an important power move strategy in any position, but they can become a winning tactic when they open a file to let a rook or queen pile up on a pinned piece. A pawn break is a special kind of pawn move that forces a pawn trade, leading to an open file. Here's a common pawn break on move two!
1.e4 e5 2.f4

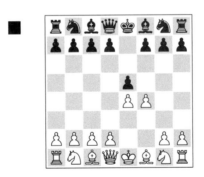

King's Gambit

A successful pawn break usually requires two pawns that 'butt heads together', like the white pawn on e4 and the black one on e5. White can then play the 'levers' 2.f4 or 2.d4, forcing Black to either capture, or let White take him next move, because the 'headbutter' pawn on e4 prevents Black from advancing his e-pawn to stop the trade.

The word 'lever' was used by the Austrian master Hans Kmoch in his famous book, *Pawn Power in Chess* – a great book about pawn play for advanced players. If you pull a lever on a machine it makes something happen – and it's the same with a pawn lever! This action move creates excitement and tension on the board.

If 2...exf4 White usually plays 3.♘f3 (stopping the dangerous 3...♕h4+) and continues with ♗c4, 0-0, and d4. If White can regain the pawn on f4, he creates a strong open file for his castled rook on f1. If not, he may sacrifice a piece to open the file, or play the further pawn break g3.

Levers can answer a key question asked by kids everywhere: how can I activate my rooks? We've seen how rooks love open files, and a good pawn break forces open a file. Remember this power move idea!

In the following dinosaur game the 'King's Gambit' f4 lever was used decisively a little bit later:

Daniels-Walker (variation), London 1841

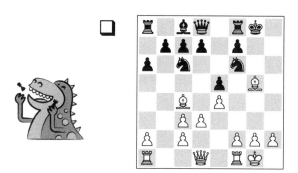

White has played a common knight sacrifice for two pawns and a vicious pin of the ♘f6. On 1.♕f3 Black can defend for the moment with 1...♔g7, but the pawn break **1.f4!** wins quickly. The f-file is pried open and White regains the knight with a pile-up.

A sample line is **1...♔g7 2.fxe5 ♘xe5 3.♗xf6+**, winning the queen for rook and knight, plus retaining two extra pawns and an attack on Black's king. A killer pawn break!

In the next example, White missed a deadly pawn break allowing a pile-up on an absolute diagonal pin.

Gulko-Karpov, Dos Hermanas 1994

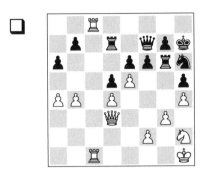

GM Boris Gulko, the only player ever to win both the US and Russian Championships, missed the winning lever **1.g4!**. White threatens 2.gxh5 with a pile-up on the pinned ♖g6, and after 1...♘xg4 (or 1...hxg4 2.h5) 2.♘xg4 hxg4 3.h5! the break has freed the h-pawn for the winning pile-up.

Black must try **1...f5** to break the pin, when the strongest response is **2.g5!**.

position after 2.g5

Here's a very unusual situation that teaches a new concept: a **positional win**! The black g6 rook is imprisoned by his own pawns and White's, and can never escape.

In effect, White is a rook ahead, and he can win easily with moves like ♕c3 and ♖c7, trading off all black defenders and invading on the queenside, while the ♖g6 looks on helplessly.

Here's a recent example of a power move pawn break creating a winning pile-up pin:
(see next page)

V. Karnic-Dean (variation), Plainville 2009

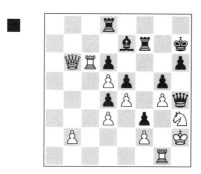

Black has an absolute pin on the ♘h3, but how can he exploit it? The only way is the tremendous power move **1...h5!**.

This fantastic lever threatens the pile-up 2...hxg4; for instance 2.♖c7 hxg4 3.♖xg4 (3.♖xe7 ♕xh3#) 3...♕xg4

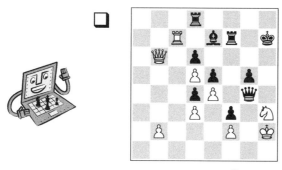

analysis after 3...♕xg4

4.♖xe7 ♕g2#!

So **2.gxh5** is forced in the first diagram, but then **2...g4** piles up and wins the knight with a quick win for Black.

This position shows the importance of pawn breaks. If Black didn't have the break ...h5, he would soon lose, because his attack would stall, while White has an extra pawn on the queenside and a big attack coming with ♖c7 and ♕b7.

Awesome! I always wondered how to free my rooks.

'Horizontal' Pile-Ups

Pile-up pins sometimes happen on the 'rank', or horizontal row. Here White's queen is pinning Black's knight along the 4th rank, so of course he looks for the pile-up.

Kasparov-Gicin, Riga 1977

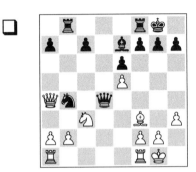

1.a3! wins a ♘ because either of Black's hook-up unpinning tries 1...♘c6 or 1...♘c2 lets White's queen take the knight for free.

Rook checks on the eighth row often lead to pile-ups if the enemy blocks the check with a piece:

Vetoshko-Kozel, Chervonograd 2008

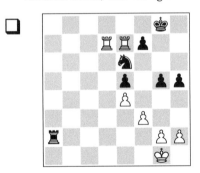

White has a good move (1.♖xf7) but finds a much better one that leads to resignation, thanks to 1.5 power move calculation:
1.♖e8+!
With his board sight White alertly notices that on 1...♔g7 2.♖xe6! wins the knight due to the pinned f-pawn, while **1...♘f8** allows the double rook pile-up **2.♕dd8** vacuuming up the ♘.

Pile-Up Pins: Exercises

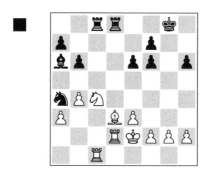

Snag a piece with a perfect pile-up pin.

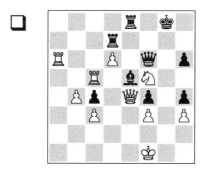

Force a win with a horizontal pile-up.

Pile-Up Pins: Solutions

Kozul-Kasparov, Belgrade 1989

Seeing the ♘c4 is pinned to the ♖c1, Garry pounces by piling up with the cheapest unit:

1...b5! gets a free ♘.

Tiviakov-Elianov, Montreal 2007

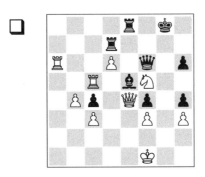

White's ♕ is lined up with the ♖e8, but it also pins Black's ♗.

The pile-up **1.♖aa5!** overwhelms the pinned bishop (use your quick count!).

A bit more complicated was 1.♘e7+ (interfering with the ♖e8's defense of the bishop – we study more **interference moves** in Chapter 5) 1...♖7xe7 and now 2.♕xc4+! ♖/♕e6 3.d7! also wins.

Pin-Exploiting Moves #2:
The Sneaky Pin

Learning this trick will make you a tactical tiger! A **sneaky pin** is a situation where a piece or key square *looks* protected, but really isn't because of a pin! Your piece is able to occupy the 'impossible' square for a quick win! I also call this power move tactic an 'optical illusion' pin, meaning it fools your eyes. Finding sneaky pins requires extra good board sight, so your opponent will often miss them.

Sneaky Pins 1: Captures

In these examples, a piece looks protected but really isn't, due to a sneaky pin.

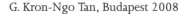

G. Kron-Ngo Tan, Budapest 2008

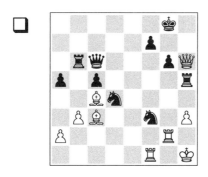

Black is trying to kick out the white queen with his rook, but there's one little problem: **1.♕xh5!** wins the rook! He forgot that the g-pawn is absolutely pinned by the ♖g2.

Serefidou-Styazhkina, Vung Tau U-12 Girls, 2008

In this game from a kids' tournament, White thought her extra kingside pawns could shelter the king, but she missed the power of the bishop's sneaky pin on the a7-g1 diagonal!

1...♛xg3+!

The pawn's protection was only an optical illusion. The absolute pin on the f-pawn spells mate!

2.♔h1 ♛xh3# (or 2...♛g2#)

Alert attacking play by Anna Styazhkina!

Mnatsakanian-A. Zaitsev, Yerevan 1962

Black thinks his knights protect each other, but his eyes are deceiving him! After **1.♛xe4! ♞xe4 2.♗xa5** White has won a knight, thanks to the sneaky pin.

Kolisch-Gastein, Vienna 1859

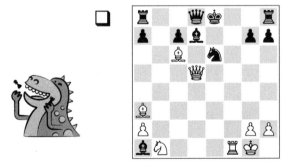

It looks like Black's knight is protected, but use your board sight:

1.♛xe6+ and Black is done: **1...♛e7** (forced because of the sneaky-pinned ♗d7) **2.♛xe7** checkmate!

'Sneaky Pin' Piece Captures: Exercises

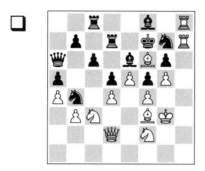

Is the knight really protected?

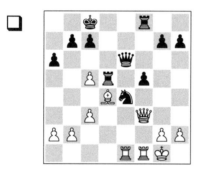

Use a sneaky pin and 1.5+ power move calculation!

'Sneaky Pin' Piece Captures: Solutions

Forintos-Hansson, Esbjerg 1983

1.♗xg7! and the eighth-rank sneaky pin prevents recapturing (1...♗xg7 2.♖xc8).

L. Paulsen-Fritz, Breslau 1889

1.♖xe4! stole the ♘ because the f-pawn is pinned: **1...♕xe4 2.♕xe4 fxe4 3.♖xf8+**

Sneaky Pins 2:
Square Invasions

Masters don't overlook sneaky-pinned piece captures too often, but even they miss enemy pieces entering key attacking squares that look guarded, but aren't thanks to a sneaky pin. It's easier to notice that your piece is attacked, than to see that a key *square* is left open. But these sneaky square invasions can be just as powerful as taking a piece, often leading to big material gain or mate!

Naiditsch-Carlsen, Wijk aan Zee 2006

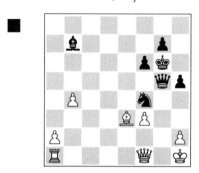

Magnus is down an exchange and a pawn, but he sees that his queen can enter a crushing square that looks off-limits. The sneaky invasion **1...♕g4!** exploits the ♗b7's absolute pin on the f-pawn to threaten the killer check 2...♗xf3+. If 2.h3 ♕g3! closes the white ♔'s air hole on h2; 3.♗xf4 ♗xf3+ 4.♕xf3 ♕xf3+ and 5...♕xf4 wins the queen for just a rook, so White resigned.

F. Bruno-Van den Bersselaar, Gibraltar 2009

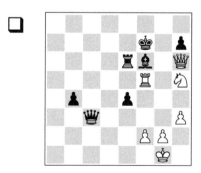

Instead of just taking the h-pawn, White uses the paralysis of the pinned ♗f6 to enter an 'impossible' square and pry the black king from the defense of his bishop: **1.♕g7+!** wins instantly.

Morphy-NN, New Orleans 1850

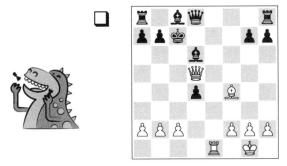

Paul Morphy, 'the king of the dinosaurs', was famed as a deadly attacker, but he was also way ahead of his peers in understanding positions, and was great at endgames. Here, access to a sneaky key square led to a pretty mate in 3:

1.♕c5+! ♔b8

1...♔d7 2.♕xd6#.

2.♕xd6+ ♕xd6 3.♗xd6#

Check Moves Takes Takes Bang!

Right-o! If you can see that far ahead, your opponents are toast.

Isn't this earth-object a cooked piece of bread?

Yeah right, Zort, just pop your opponent in the toaster! LOL!

Ehlvest-Kasparov, Moscow 1977

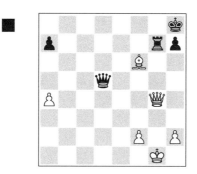

This position shows Kasparov's incredible board sight. Super grandmaster Jaan Ehlvest probably thought he would win here. True, his queen is pinned to the ♔ by the ♖g7, but strangely, the pinning rook is also caught in an absolute pin by the ♗f6!

If 1...♕f7 2.♕xg7+ trades off all the pieces, and White wins with his extra pawn. But Garry saw far in advance that White's attack is an optical illusion: the monster sneaky pin **1...♕d1+!!** wins the paralyzed queen and mates in two more moves!

Here's a very common and important power move based on a sneaky pin:

Strunsky-Michna, Deizisau 2008

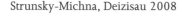
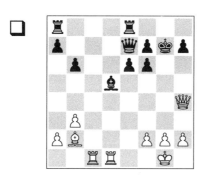

Black has enough defenders of his crucial f6 pawn, but not for long:
1.♕g5+!
The ♔ must retreat due to the sneaky-pinned ♙f6:
1...♔f8 2.♗xf6 and Black must give the queen to stop 3.♕g7#.

Let's not forget one of the most important sneaky-pin mates.

R. Bauer-Bryan, New England Open 1997

If you showed this problem to ten kids in your school, I bet only one or two at most would find the solution! It's really just a Takes Takes Bang! idea, but you need great board sight to consider the forcing queen sacrifice, and then notice the winning sneaky pin. Bobby Fischer included this idea in his neat little book, *Bobby Fischer Teaches Chess*.

Black wasn't worried so much about 1.♗xf7+? ♔h8! (but not 1...♖xf7 2.♖d8+ and mate) when Black threatens back rank mate, the rook and the c5 pawn. After 2.♖e4! White is still better but Black may hold. But he missed a much more forcing move and learned a new master stock checkmate using a sneaky pin:

1.♕xf7+! ♖xf7 2.♖d8#!

The sneaky-pinned ♖f7 can't interpolate. Remember this beautiful mate that seems to explode onto the board out of nowhere! It shows how strong a sneaky pin can be.

By the way, a 'stock checkmate' is one that occurs over and over in master play, though it may be very beautiful and surprising when you first see it! My adult chess book *Forcing Chess Moves* has two chapters on stock master mates, and many other fine books have been written just about them. After you've learned all the master tactics in *Power Chess* Book One and Book Two, studying more of these mates would be a great next step!

Sneaky-Pin Square Invasions: Exercises

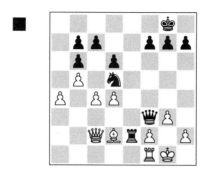

A very sneaky square attack – look closely!

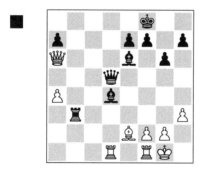

Use a sneaky pin to invade an 'impossible' square for quick checkmate.

Sneaky-Pin Square Invasions: Solutions

Mahescandra-Cochrane, Calcutta 1851

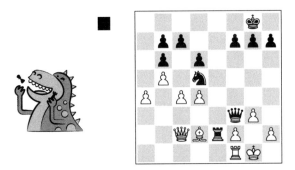

A **double pin** lets Black enter an off-limits square – and attack everything in sight! These two dinosaurs played hundreds of games against each other in the 1850's. The more famous Cochrane won most of the games, but his dangerous Indian opponent also scored some beautiful wins.

Black found **1...♘e3!** forking the ♕&♖ and threatening mate on g2! White resigned because the two relative pins will cost him his queen: 2.♗xe3 (2.fxe3 ♕g2#) 2...♖xc2.

Bareev-Kasparov, Paris rapid 1991

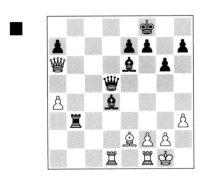

In this rapid-play game, a powerful super-grandmaster overlooked Black's 'sneaky-pin access' to a key mating square:

1...♖g3! threatens 2...♕xg2#. The pinned f-pawn's defense of g3 is an optical illusion, and if 2.♗f3 ♕xf3! the white g2 pawn is now pinned and paralyzed as well! Mate is coming, so White gave up.

Paralyzing Pins

Some pins are so strong and unbreakable, they dominate the whole position. Here are a few examples of these super pins, including the famous 'eternal pin':

Horwitz-Harrwitz, London 1846

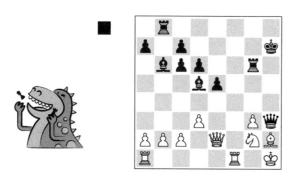

Black's two powerful bishops rake White's kingside and pin the ♘, while the sorry ♗h2 is also pinned.

Black piles up with **1...♖h6** and White resigns, pinned to death!

Nijboer-Solodovnichenko, Utrecht 2009

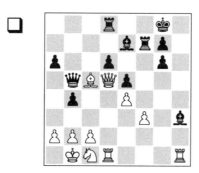

This one is so pretty, let's wake Zort up and see the computer-eye view:

Yes master Hertan, I'm sure that earth kids will love this beautiful paralyzing pin mate. **1.♖xh3!**, taking the bishop, was a great power move, because Black's answer appears to win White's queen, but White had looked deeper.

1...dxc5! This discovers an attack on White's queen, which can't move away without losing the rook on d1. On 2.♕xd8+ ♗d8 3.♖xd8+ ♖f8, accurate two move calculation shows that White gets just rook and bishop for the ♕, not enough! So, has White made a big mistake?

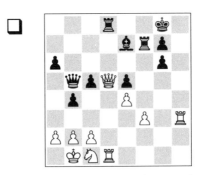

Position after 1...dxc5: is the queen lost?

2.♖dh1!!

A four-star power move! White has foreseen that the loss of his queen doesn't matter – she pins the ♖f7 just long enough to prevent Black's king from escaping mate on h8.

Black resigned due to **2...♖xd5 3.♖h8#**.

'Eternal Pins'

Eternal means forever. Some absolute pins are so strong, they can *never* be broken without loss of material or mate. Such a monster pin almost always wins.

Sarkar-Barros Lizcano, Boca Raton 2008

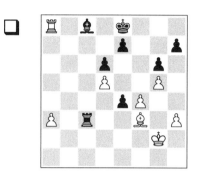

White has a much stronger idea than recapturing the pawn:
1.♗g4! ♚d8
Forced, to protect the bishop.
2.♗e6
This move wasn't strictly necessary, but it illustrates Black's helplessness. There is no way for him to escape the pin without losing his bishop! 2...♚c7 allows 3.♖xc8+, winning the bishop as well as skewering and winning the rook! So Black's king is glued to d8, while his rook is glued to the c-file. The white king can stop the e-pawn, and then White pushes his a-pawn all the way up to make a queen, since all three black pieces are stuck!
I can't blame Black for committing *harakiri* with **2...♖f3 3.♖xc8#**.

Henrichs-Op den Kelder, Maastricht 2009

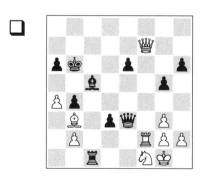

White's extra knight doesn't mean a thing here, because the absolute pins on the back rank and the a7-g1 diagonal tie White in knots! White out-rated his opponent by 235 points, but resigned because ...d2 is coming, e.g. 1.♕f3 (Black was also threatening the power move combo 1...♖xf1+! 2.♔xf1 ♕c1+ and mate) 1...d2! 2.♕xe3 ♗xe3 and neither pinned white piece can take the pawn; or 1.♕xe6+ ♕xe6 2.♗xe6 ♖c2, a decisive pile-up pin.

Here's the best example ever of an eternal pin.

J. Kaplan-Bronstein, Hastings 1975/76

You and me can understand this position better than any computer!

Oh yeah??

Sorry Zort, but it's true! You see, computers are the best at calculating variations, but there's one thing we're great at that they can't do: coming up with great ideas that sometimes let us understand the whole position without calculating variations.

Duh, great ideas: that's how we *invented* computers, right?

You invented us? But I was told my father's hard drive interfaced with my mother's software, and that's how I was born. Excuse me, I have some research to do.

Anyway... we can use our great human ideas to solve this position. The rook on d2 is pinned by the bishop, and neither the white king nor ♖d1 can make any moves that don't lose the rook for nothing. If we can keep him boxed up like that, he will only have pawn moves left, and when he runs out of those, bye bye rook!

Here's the hard part – can you see how White might try to escape the pin? If it were his move he plays 1.c4!, then 2.c3 and 3.♔c2. So Black just prevents this with **1...c4!**

A strong human knows this wins, but a computer doesn't yet! He can only evaluate the position by computing variations, so he has to look at 1.a3, 1.a4, 1.h3, 1.h4, etc., and all Black's replies, and eventually he figures it out the hard way! But Kaplan resigned, because after say 1.a4 a5 2.g4 ♗e3 3.h4 h6 the rook falls in a few more moves.

Pin-Busters

We've explored all different kinds of pins, so now you know why pins are the most dangerous master tactic. But in case you start thinking that pins make winning easy, we must mention that not all pins are decisive, or even strong! Often pins can be **broken** by capturing the pinning piece, interposing a piece between the pinner and the pinned, or in the case of relative pins, by moving the pinned piece anyway to create a **counter-threat**.

For instance, in the French Defense **1.e4 e6 2.d4 d5**, after **3.♘c3** the sharpest line for Black is the Winawer Variation **3...♗b4**, pinning the knight which defends White's e-pawn.

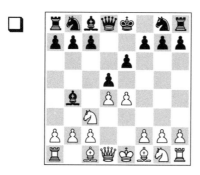

Winawer French: 3...♗b4

But if White instead plays the strong Tarrasch Variation **1.e4 e6 2.d4 d5 3.♘d2**, now the pin **3...♗b4?** would be a very weak move:

Tarrasch French: 3...♗b4?

The pin is bad here, because White easily breaks it with the **interpolation 4.c3!**. Not only is the black ♗ attacked and forced to move again, but White gets in the very useful move c3 'for free', supporting his center and opening a diagonal for the queen. In fact, this strong **pin-buster** is the whole point of Tarrasch's variation 3.♘d2, supporting the center pawn while avoiding Winawer's pin.

A good example of escaping a relative pin by moving the pinned piece *anyway* to make a stronger threat is the famous Legal's Mate:

1.e4 e5 2.♘f3 d6 3.♗c4 ♗g4?!
It's dangerous to play this pinning move here because it delays castling and developing the knights longer than usual.
4.♘c3 h6??
But this move leads to disaster. In the opening, *every move* should help you develop your bishops and knights and castle! This move does nothing to help Black mobilize. White is already able to punish the mistake with powerful pin-buster tactics, sacrificing his queen!

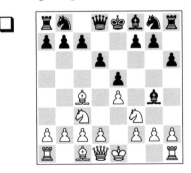

5.♘xe5! ♗xd1?
Better is 5...dxe5 6.♕xg4, but then White has won a pawn with a great position.
6.♗xf7+ ♚e7 7.♘d5#

Legal's Mate

Problem composers call this an 'ideal mate', because each of the king's 5 escape squares is guarded by only one piece.

For you, it's a good reminder that relative pins can sometimes be ignored, to make a stronger threat like mate.

Here are a few more neat examples where players escaped pins and turned the tables. If someone catches you in a dangerous pin, don't give up – look for power moves!

Meitner-Blackburne, Vienna 1873

The ♗e6 is pinned, but Black escapes with 1.5 power move calculation:
1...♕f6!
Threatens 2...♕xb2# and unpins the ♗e6, so Black kept his extra piece.

L. Paulsen-Steinitz, Vienna 1873

1...h5! forced the white ♕ to give up the absolute pin on the knight, and the extra black ♘ got away.

Cool power move! But I'm still going to use lots of pins in my games from now on!

Great idea! That's the best way to learn power moves, and win more games while you're at it.

Pin-Busters: Exercises

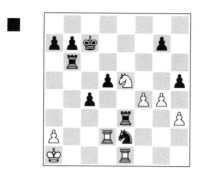

Why did the sixth World Champion Botvinnik, playing with black, allow a pile-up pin of his ♘e2?

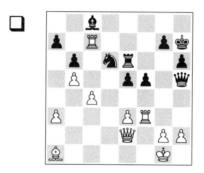

A tough one! Win the ♕, or checkmate in four with the two rooks.

Pin-Busters: Solutions

Lilienthal-Botvinnik, Moscow 1945

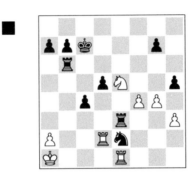

The great champion Mikhail Botvinnik used 1.5 power move calculation to find a winning pin-buster.

1...♘c3! escapes the pin due to **2.♖xe3 ♖b1#!** White resigned since he is down two pawns with no good moves.

Ding Liren-Li Shilong, Xinghua Jiangsu 2010

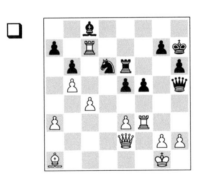

The values show White has a winning edge, but being up the exchange can be tough to cash in. White found a brilliant pin-buster that made Black resign.

1.♖g3! ♕xe2

Black might as well take the queen; if 1...♕e8 2.♖3xg7+ the white ♖'s are too strong.

2.♖cxg7+! ♔h8 3.♖g8+ ♔h7 4.♖3g7#!

This stock master 'double rook mate' is a great one to remember! Play it over a few times so you'll remember it for future use.

Chapter 4

Skewers

'**Move out of my way, enemy piece, so I can take your friend!**'

A skewer is like a pin turned inside out.

Pin

In this position the rook is pinned to the king. White wins the exchange after 1...♔f7.

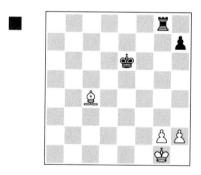

Skewer

Here we say the king and rook are **skewered** on the diagonal. The king must move, and then the bishop will take the rook, which becomes exposed on the same line. Notice that in this case, the skewer is even stronger than the pin – White wins a whole rook.

So, if we put these diagrams into words – in the case of the pin, the rook **can't move** because it's pinned to the king, so White wins rook for bishop. In the case of the skewer, the king **has to move** (because it's in check), which then exposes the piece behind it to capture.

Have you ever eaten the famous middle eastern food, shish kebab? It's a delicious dish with cubes of meat and vegetables grilled on a straight stick. The stick that runs through the juicy morsels is called a skewer. So when you skewer two or more enemy pieces on the same line, it's like making shish kebab on the chess board! As with pins, the three pieces that move as far as they want on a straight line are the only chessmen that can make a skewer: bishop, rook, and queen.

Bishop Skewers

Kasparov-Beliavsky, Reggio Emilia 1991/92

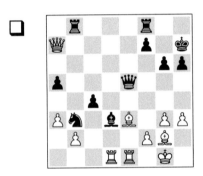

The skewer **1.♗f4!** wins the exchange after 1...♕b5 2.♗xb8, so Black gave up.

Purnama-Zhang Zhong, Tarakan 2008

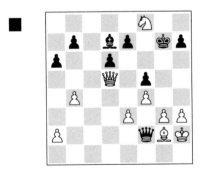

White has just taken a rook on f8, but Black noticed something very important. Instead of recapturing the knight, he has a better move. In my book *Forcing*

Chess Moves I call this an equal or stronger threat ('EST' for short). The skewer **1...♗c6! 2.♘e6+ ♔g8!** wins the queen, because if 3.♕d4 ♕xg2 is mate. Good 1.5 power move calculation, eh?

Good board sight, too!

Stanley-Rousseau, New Orleans 1845

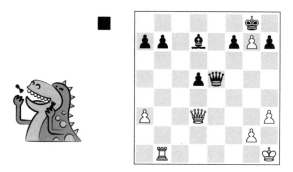

Black regained the exchange with **1...♗f5! 2.♕b3 ♗xb1 3.♕xb1 b6** and was soon up two pawns for nothing.

Cochrane-Mahescandra, Calcutta 1854

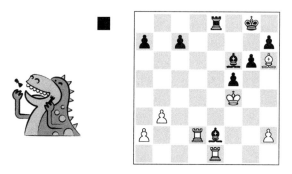

A good moment for the Indian dinosaur; he found a Check Moves Bang! combination ending in a bishop skewer:
1...♖e4+ 2.♔g3 ♗h4+ winning a rook.

Petrov-Von Jaenisch, St. Petersburg 1844

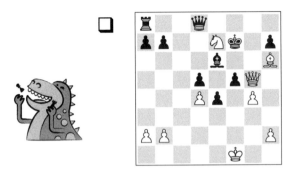

Another Check Moves Bang! skewer wins the queen by sacking a knight:

1.♕h5+! ♔xe7

If 1...♔f6 2.♗g5+ ♔g7 3.♘xf5+, the queen falls anyway.

2.♗g5+, a 'royal skewer' of ♔+♕.

Rook Skewers

Since rook checks on the back rank are so common, skewers often happen there.

Blass-Friedmann, Lodz 1927

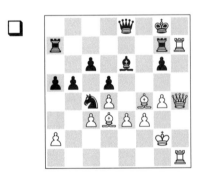

White converted a crushing attack on the h-file with a ♖ 'skew':

1.♖h8+ ♔f7 2.♖xe8.

Prieto Azuar-Falcon Lugo, San Juan 1971

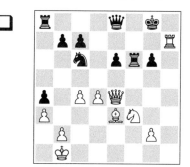

Black is up the exchange, but **1.♕h4!** threatens to skewer the queen or give mate. Black's goose is cooked, so he resigned.

What if 1...g5? Oops, I see it: 2.♖h8+ ♔f7 3.♕h7#. Never mind!

Nice job! Check Moves Bang!

Why is Black cooking a goose? Is he making shish kebab?

Oh, shush Zort, I'll tell you later.

Schmidt-Barle, Pula 1975

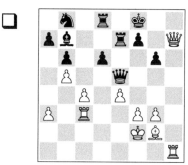

Seeing that Black's queen attacks the ♗c3, many kids would move the rook first and ask questions later! I call this 'knee-jerk defense': defending without checking for better moves. Instead, analyze the forcing check **1.♕h8+!**: White trades queens, then skewers a whole rook in 1.5 power moves!

Dobrov-I. Almasi, Oberwart 2000

Here's another important idea; White uses a mate threat to catch the loose black rook in a skewer:

1.♖d2! White is already up the exchange, but now he wins a lot more with this forcing move attacking the ♗.

1...♗e6 2.♖2h2!

Threatening the stock double-rook mate 3.♖h8+ and 4.♖2h7#. Black can escape with 2...♔f8, but 3.♖h8+ skewers a whole rook.

White had other winning possibilities with the same theme: 1.♖h3, or 1.♔b2 and 2.♖g1 – but not 1.♖g1?? right away because of the knight fork 1...♘e2+.

The seventh row is the other best place for a rook skewer:

Metger-Tarrasch, Frankfurt 1887

Black finds a better move than recapturing the knight:

1...⌐b1+!

The passed pawn on the 7th row limits White's options – he must take or it queens.

2.⌐xd2 ⌐b2+! 0-1

Carlsen-Ivanchuk, Nice 2010

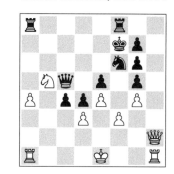

In this instructive example a check on the back row forces White into a skewer on Black's seventh row. The winner is the great Ukrainian GM Vassily Ivanchuk.

1...♕xb5!! 2.axb5 ⌐xa1+ 3.⌐f2 ⌐a2+ White regains the queen with an extra piece.

You know by now that rooks don't only gobble things on the back rows – they also love to invade on open files! Here are some typical **vertical skewers**:

T. Reiter-Radfar, Vienna 2008

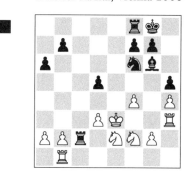

A vertical skewer piles up on the e2 knight and wins:

1...⌐e8+! 0-1

Lupor-Naumann, Bad Wiessee 2008

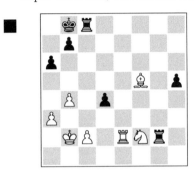

Another vertical skewer by the rook; this time without a check: **1...♖f8!**

Welling-Bronstein, Bussum 1991

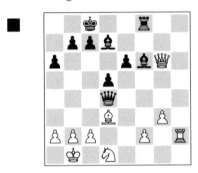

Here's a tricky one. Remember we said that moving backwards is sometimes the strongest power move? Grandmaster Bronstein proved it here:
1...♗e8! 2.♕h6
The queen has to go on the h-file because 2.c3 ♗xg6 3.cxd4 ♗xd3+ wins.
2...♖h8!
A winning skewer! A quick count shows the rook is double-protected by the ♗ and ♕, and 3.♗h7? allows 3...♖xh7! 4.♕xh7? ♕xd1#.

Queen Skewers

Yes, the mighty queen is great at skewers too! She can skewer pieces on the file, rank, or diagonal, giving her twice the chances of a rook or bishop!

The queen loves back-rank skewers just like the rook, because the enemy king is often found there. In the next examples, the grandmaster lures the opposing queen into position for a crushing skewer on the eighth row:

Bareev-Morozevich (variation), Moscow 2005

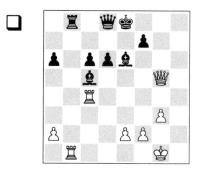

1.♖xb8!
White's ♕ is protected by the sneaky pin.
1...♕xb8 2.♕g8+.
A nice Takes Takes Bang! idea. Interestingly, reversing the move order doesn't work: 1.♕g8+? ♔d7 2.♖xb8 (2.♕xd8+ ♖xd8) 2...♕xg8 3.♖xg8 ♗xc4 with a win for Black!

Here's a simple but beautiful 1.5 power move combination that is easy to miss because it is very creative – you must use your imagination to even consider the winning first move, which seems to just lose a rook.

Li Chao-Xu Jun, Beijing 2009

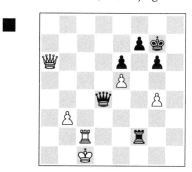

1...♖f1+!! 2.♕xf1 ♕a1+ bags the queen! Because of dangerous checks like this, king safety is a big advantage in queen and rook endgames.

This is the clearest and most forcing win for Black. This is what we mean by good board sight: seeing what all the pieces can do, and not forgetting a power move like 1...♖f1+!! just because it looks impossible! Use your imagination to come up with neat possibilities like this.

Kasparov-Hübner, Hamburg 1985

It starts with a simple back rank skewer:
1.♕h8+ ♔f7 2.♕xd8

But why did the German super-GM Hübner resign now, when he can take back a piece three ways?
Answer: winning power moves in every line!

Kasparov-Hübner after 2.♕xd8

A) 2...♔xg6 3.♗h5+ ♔h6 3.♗f7#;
B) 2...♖xg6 3.♖h7+ ♔e6 (or 3...♖g7 4.♗h5+ and mate) 4.♕e8+ skewers the ♕; but even stronger is 4.♕d7+ or 4.♕c8+ with mate in 4;
C) 2...♕xd1 3.♘e5+ (also 3.♘h8+) 3...♔e6 4.♖h6+ mates.

Wish I could calculate like Garry!

I can.

Oh yeah? Well, I can eat your microprocessors for lunch.

OK, settle down guys! Don't forget: it all starts with seeing 1.5 power moves ahead.

Queen skewers on the 7th row are also very common.

Levin-Dvoretsky, Kharkov 1967

A beautiful 2.5 power move combination sets up a winning skewer:
1.♘d7!!
A good try, but not good enough, is 1.♖h7+ ♘xh7 2.♕xh7+ ♔f6! 3.♘d7+ ♔g5. But now Black resigns!
The threat is 2.♖h7+ ♘xh7 3.♕xh7#. If 1...♘xd7 2.♖h7#, but on **1...♕xd7 2.♖h7+ ♘xh7 3.♕xh7+** is a queen-wins-queen skewer.

Chigorin-Zukertort, London 1883

White's king has taken a bad walk into no-man's land. One way to win would be the pile-up pin 1...c5, but Black chooses a crisp skewer trick winning the queen: **1...♖xd4+ 2.♔xd4 ♕g4+**

Did you notice that the ♗b7 prevents 3.♖e4?

I noticed. My planet Zugzwang is also *no-man's land*: only computers live there.

Well, duh! He wasn't talking to you, silly! Everyone knows you have perfect computer board sight. But I can kick your butt in football! Hah!

Diagonal Queen Skewers

Here's another queen skewer on the back rank – but this time a diagonal one.

Rousseau-Kolisch, Paris 1867

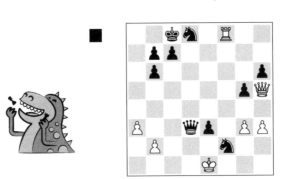

1...♕b1+
Notice how the advanced e-pawn helps Black's attack! Forced is **2.♔e2 ♕d1+!** spearing the queen on the diagonal.

Zhou Weiqi-Yu Yangyi, Beijing 2009

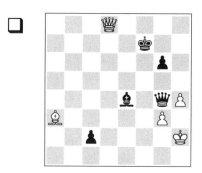

White finds a Check Moves Bang! combination to force Black into a winning diagonal skewer:

1.♕f8+ ♔e6 2.♕c8+! 1-0

Winning the ♕ was great, but White missed checkmate: 1.♕e7+! ♔g8 2.♕f8+ ♔h7 3.♕f7+ ♔h6 (3...♔h8 4.♗b2#) 4.♗f8+ ♔h5 5.♕h8#.

Skewers are also called **x-ray attacks** because they seem to attack one piece right through another! Most books don't mention this, but there's also such a thing as an 'x-ray defense':

Stefanova-Peptan, Moscow 1995

Did you spot White's deadly threat 1.♕h7#? Black found a fantastic move that defends h7 right 'through' White's queen, and makes winning counterthreats!

1...♕b1!! 2.♕e2

The black queen captures on 2.♕g6+ or 2.♕h7+, and the back-rank deflection 2.♕xb1 ♖f1 is mate.

2...♕d1!

Another **deflection** move forces White to resign, because she can't defend both the f1 mate square and the bishop. More deflections are coming in Book 2.

Bashilin-Podzielny (variation), Essen 2000

X-ray defenses aren't only good for stopping the opponent's threat – they're also a good way to protect your own attackers. Black can't avoid checkmate here due to the ♗f6's x-ray defense of the key h8-square. The biggest threat is **1.♕h8+!! ♗xh8 2.♖xh8#**, and on 1...♗xf6 2.exf6, mate on h8 is coming anyway.

Here's a very cool queen sac version of the same common master tactic:

Nilsson-Henriksen, Copenhagen 1996

The stellar power move **1.♕f6!!** forces mate, thanks to the ♕'s x-ray pressure on h8. Notice that 2.♖h8+ is threatened, and the king can't walk away: 1...♗xf6 2.gxf6 ♔f8 3.♖h8#.

Skewers: Exercises

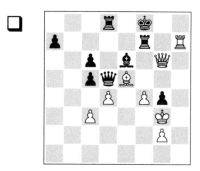

Two skewers lead to mate.

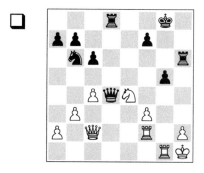

Find a winning vertical skewer.

Skewers: Solutions

Weissgerber-Schmitt, Aachen 1934

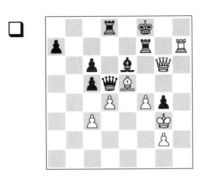

Black resigned before White could play his crushing 'one-two punch': a rook skewer, a queen skewer, and mate!

1.♖h8+ ♔e7 2.♕g5+ ♔d7 3.♕xd8#

Uusi-Kalashian, Moscow 1959

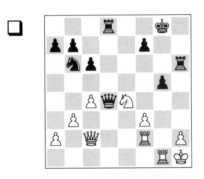

1.♖d2! was a typical skewer trap by the rook on an open file. The key ♘e4 protects the ♖ and prevents the defense 1...♕f6, so Black loses the queen or the rook.

Skewers: Exercises

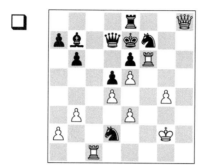

A 'skewer trick'-sacrifice to win.

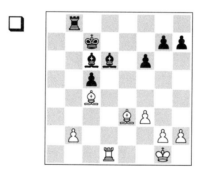

Takes Takes Bang!

Skewers: Solutions

Parr-Broadbent, Nottingham 1946

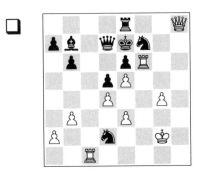

Black is up a lot of material: 3 minor pieces for a rook. White better have something good up his sleeve, and he does, a winning skewer trick:

1.♖xf7+! ♔xf7

On 1...♔d8 the queen falls *with check*.

2.♕h7+ 1-0

Nakamura-S. Muhammad, San Diego 2004

The game looks even, but the young American super GM has foreseen a winning skewer trick: **1.♖xd6!** (Takes) **1...♔xd6** (Takes) **2.♗f4+** (Bang!) emerging with an extra bishop!

Nothing is changed by 1...♖b4 2.♗f4! ♖xc4 3.♖d4+! – a winning **discovered check** which we will cover in *Book 2*.

Chapter 5

Interference Moves

'Sorry buddy, you can't stop my threat: I'll step in your way!'

You've mastered the first three master tactics, and are ready to try them out in your games! The pin, fork and skewer are sometimes called the 'geometric tactics'. The moves of the chessmen all make different shapes or patterns (like straight lines, diagonals, or L-shapes), and the first three tactics are based on the way each piece moves. (We call them 'geometric' because geometry is the branch of math that deals with shapes.)

Lots of kids' books only cover the geometric tactics, but we will go much further and cover *all* the tactical tricks that win games. These advanced master tactics aren't really based on the geometry of the pieces; they are more about special ideas that can be used by any piece (except the king!) to sacrifice itself for mate or material gain.

The first advanced master tactic we will study is the **interference move**. These moves *put one of your pieces in the way of an enemy piece,* so it can't stop you from checkmating or winning material. Usually this involves a surprising sacrifice. If you notice that only one enemy piece prevents you from doing something great, there are several things you can try to get past it. The simplest ways are chasing it away or trading it off, and if you can do that, great. But often there's no easy way to get rid of a key defender, so you will have to consider two tactics – the interference move, or the **deflection sacrifice**, which we consider in Book 2.

Peptan-Genzling, Kallithea 2008

When the other girl has a weak back rank, almost any power move tactic may be the right one to break through. White's strong doubled rooks can't do the job themselves, because e8 is protected twice. But White sees the flaw in Black's defenses; the bishop taking on e8 will interfere with the black ♖'s protection of f8, letting the white ♕ fly in:

1.♖e8+! ♗xe8 2.♕f8#! (or 1...♖xe8 2.♖xe8+ ♗xe8 3.♕f8#)

Always look out for such shocking power moves when only one enemy piece stops back-rank mate!

Lushovsky-Griedner, USSR 1976

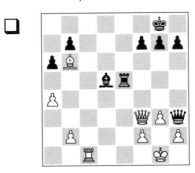

Black hoped to win White's queen here. She can't move due to 1...♕g2#. But White saw that only the black ♕ defends against 1.♖c8#, and he found an interference move so stunning that Black never saw it coming: **1.g4!!** and Black must lose his queen to stop back row mate (e.g., 1...h6 2.♕xh3).

OMG! That's the *craziest* power move ever!!

Zukertort-Steinitz, London 1883

These two heavy-hitting dinosaurs slugged it out in a long match for the world championship. Here Black saw that on 1...♛e1+, White must interpose with 2.♛g1. So Black puts his pawn in the way of the white ♛:

1...b6! renews the mate threat, while stopping the defense 2.♛a5. **2.♚g1 ♛e1#** is still back rank mate, so White resigned.

G. Szabo-Anderssen, London 1851

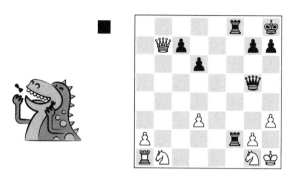

One more example where a simple pawn push interfered with the queen's defense: **1...d5! 2.g4** (else mate on g2) **2...♛f4** mating on h2 next!

Simagin-Novotelnov, Moscow 1951

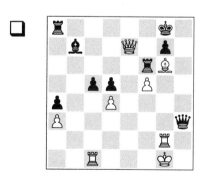

Here White's mating chances are against the g7 pawn instead of the back rank. White sees that by moving his bishop he threatens 2.♛xg7# by uncovering an attack by the ♖g2, but where to go? If 1.♗h7+, 1...♛xh7! protects against the mate, and 1.♗e8 allows 1...♛h6!.

But the interference sac **1.♗h5!** *gets in the way* of the queen's defenses! Black resigns because 1...♛xg2+, losing the queen, is the only reasonable way to stop 2.♛g7#.

De La Bourdonnais-McDonnell, London 1834

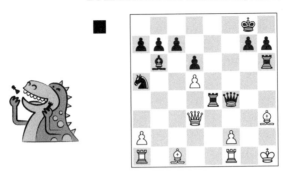

How did poor White end up four pawns down and under a mating attack? Well, the dinosaurs didn't like to resign, and White is trying to win back the exchange with the skewer ♗c1.

But the crushing bomb **1...♖e3!** (or 1...♗e3!) interferes with the white ♕'s protection of the ♗h3 and mates fast: **2.fxe3 ♖xh3+ 3.♔g2 ♕h2#**

Take that, queen!

As you can see, interference moves usually work best when only one enemy piece is stopping your *very big threat*.

Saint Amant-Morphy, Paris 1858

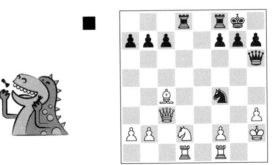

Morphy sees that only White's ♕c3 prevents 1...♕xh3+ and 2...♕g2#. He can't budge the white ♕, but finds he can put something in her way: **1...♖d3!**

'Think your ♕ stops my mate threat? Not anymore!'
2.♕xd3
Sadly forced to stop the mate.
2...♘xd3 3.♗xd3 ♕d6+ forking ♔+♗ with an easy win.

Here the white ♔ is stripped bare, and only the faraway white ♕ stops
...♕h2#. Black puts a monkey wrench in White's defense:

Kashlinskaya-Nagibin, Sochi 2009

1...♖f4! (or 1...♖e5) and even giving the queen with 2.♕xf4 only delays
...♕h2#.

Shamkovich-Visier Segovia, Palma de Mallorca 1967

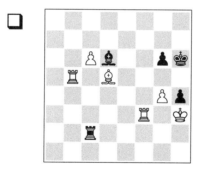

White is a whole rook up, so why doesn't Black resign? Well, look closer: Black
threatens 1...♖h2#.

After **1.g5+ ♔h5!** renews the threat by preventing the
white ♔ from escaping to g4. Is White trapped? No, he
springs a big surprise: the interference move **2.♖g3!** stops
the mate for one move, time enough for White to strike
first: **2...♗xg3 3.♗f3#!**

final position

Larsen-Tal, Leningrad 1973

Usually it's enough to interfere with a key defender, but here the interfering piece made a new threat too!

1...♖fe5!

Black cuts the white ♕'s defense of the g3 pawn, and also attacks e2

2.♔f2

2.e4 is no better; Black can take en passant, or capture two white pawns with check.

2...♖xe2+!

A Takes Takes Bang! sac leads to a crushing skewer:

3.♖xe2 ♕h2+ 4.♔f1 ♖xe2

And mate with the queen on g2 or f2. (Sorry, Zort is getting scheduled maintenance. Please play this one out, it's really good.)

So far we've seen how to create a mating attack by putting your piece in the way of an enemy defender. Interference is also used to win decisive material:

(see next page)

Short-Harikrishna, Montreal 2007

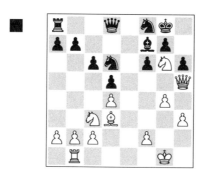

White's ♘g6 has fallen into a deadly pin by the bishop. Black could simply pile up with a third attacker and win it with 1...♕e8!, but he picked a fancier way:

1...♘e4!

Interfering with the ♗d3's protection of the ♘. White resigned because on 2.♘xe4 ♗xg6! wins a piece; if 3.♘xf6+ ♕xf6 protects the ♗ and keeps the material.

Buckle-Williams, London 1849

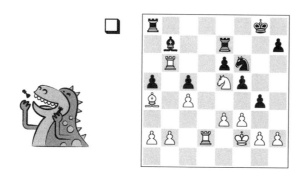

The interference move **1.♘d7!** shattered Black's defense by cutting off the ♗'s protection.

If 1...♗a6 2.♘xf6+, so Black had to take:

1...♘xd7 2.♖xb7

But now the ♘ is pinned to the rook and lost on the seventh rank.

L. Paulsen-Bird, Vienna 1873

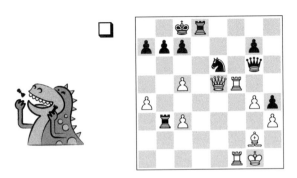

White has many ways to break Black's defenses, but can you find the strongest 1.5 power move interference shot?

1.♖f6! gxf6 2.♕xe6+

Forks ♚+♖, leaving White a piece ahead.

Bird-Rosenthal, Paris 1878

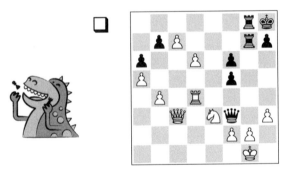

Here's a strange one: an interference move for the defense! White's pawns are poised to queen, but he must stop 1...♖xg2+ mating.

The interference move **1.♖g4!** unpins the white g-pawn so he can take the queen on 1...fxg4 2.gxf3 gxf3+ 3.♘g4.

Black resigned because 1...♖xg4 2.hxg4 or 1...♕e2 2.♖xg7 lead to a new ♕ for White.

Kasparov-Georgiev, Munich blitz, 1994

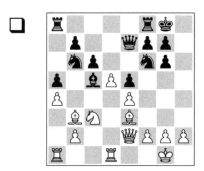

This power move uses two master tactics in one:
1.d6! won a piece by interfering with the queen's protection.
If 1...♕ moves, 2.♗xc5. Or if **1...♗xd6 2.♗xb6**, the black ♗ has been deflected from defending the knight (see Book 2!).

Interference moves have a very important role in the endgame: they are often used to *get in the way* of a key defender and force the promotion of a pawn into a queen.

Bodnaruk-Sharevich, Sochi 2009

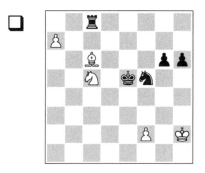

White can do even better than winning a rook with 1.a8=♕. She plays the interference idea **1.♘d7+ ♔d6 2.♘b8!** and gets to keep her new queen.

Cool, I like keeping the queen!

Nguyen Huynh Minh-Recuero Guerra, Budapest 2008

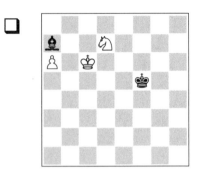

Here's a really important endgame situation. If Black could just give up his bishop for the pawn he would draw, since a lone knight can't deliver mate. The solution is to interfere with the bishop's protection of a7:

1.♔b7 ♗d4

If 1...♔e6, quickest is 2.♔xa7 ♔xd7 3.♔b7! and queens.

2.♘b6! and the pawn is home free.

Interference Moves: Exercises

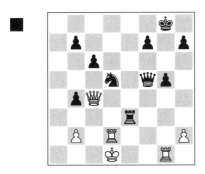

Win the queen or mate with a crisp interference sac.

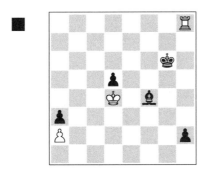

Use interference to queen a pawn.

Interference Moves: Solutions

Blackburne-Pitschel, Vienna 1873

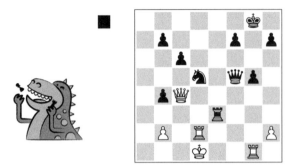

Black is winning with 4 whole pawns for the exchange, but he doesn't let White hang around, finishing him off with an interference sacrifice and an unusual back rank mate:

1...♘c3+!

On 1...♕b1+ the white ♕ can interpose with 2.♕c1, so the ♘ interferes.

2.bxc3

2.♔c1 ♕b1#; only 2.♕xc3 avoids instant mate.

2...♕b1#

Wang Jue-Zhang Xiaowen, Xinghua Jiangsu 2009

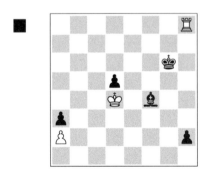

Black finishes up with the interference move **1...♗h6!** and the pawn queens. If 2.♖g8+ ♗g7+ or any king move works; the rook can't get back.

Interference Moves: Exercises

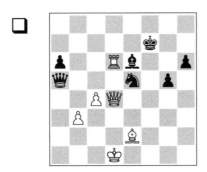

Win two pieces for a rook with a neat interference, plus a pin.

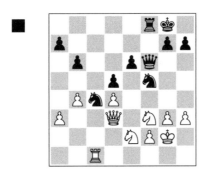

Interfere with a key defender and play for mate.

Interference Moves: Solutions

Anand-Shirov, Wijk aan Zee 2010

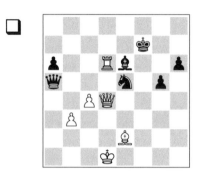

The interference shot **1.♖d5! ♗xd5 2.♕xe5!** forced Black's ♗ into a deadly pin. Black resigned because he ends up a full piece behind.

Gilg-Nimzowitsch, Karlsbad 1929

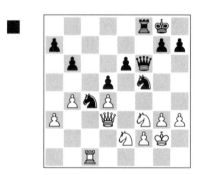

Black crashes through with **1...♘fe3+! 2.fxe3 ♕xf3+ 3.♔h2 ♘xe3** threatening 4...♕g2#, and on 4.♖g1 the discovered attack (with check!) 4...♘g4+ or 4...♘f1+ bags the queen.

Stay tuned for a whole boatload of discovered checks in Book 2.

I will – but right now I've got to go bash some opponents with all the power moves I already learned!

Chess Terms

Attack
When a piece is threatened by capture or a king is threatened by checkmate.

Back rank
The first rank (for White) or the eighth rank (for Black) on the board.

Blitz game
Quick game in which each player gets five minutes (or less) for all his moves.

Board sight
The ability to mentally envision where the pieces are, and what they can do, at each step of a calculation.

Capture
When a piece is removed by an enemy piece, which takes the place of the captured piece.

Castling
A move by king and rook that serves to bring the king into safety and to activate the rook. The king is moved sideways two squares from its original square. At the same time, a rook moves from its original square to the first square on the other side of the king.
Castling can take place either to the queenside or to the kingside. It is the only way of moving two pieces in one turn. A player may only castle if both the king and rook have not moved before, his king is not in check, and his king does not pass a square on which it will be in check.

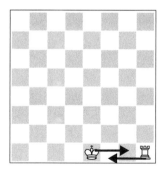

White castles kingside

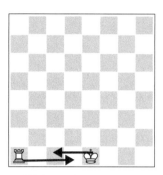

White castles queenside

Check
When a king is under direct attack by an opposing piece. A check can be countered either by moving the king, or by capturing the piece that gives the check, or by placing a piece between the king and the piece that gives check.

Checkmate
When a king is under direct attack by an opposing piece and there is no way to deal with the threat.

Combination
A clever and more or less forced sequence of moves which usually results in an advantage for the player who starts the sequence.

Cover
When a piece or a square is protected from attacks; as soon as an enemy piece captures the covered piece or occupies the covered square, it is (re)captured by the covering piece.
Also: Protect.

Deflection
When a piece is lured away from an important square, file, rank or diagonal.

Diagonal
A line of squares running from top left to bottom right or the other way round (e.g. 'the a1-h8 diagonal', 'the light-squared diagonal').

Direct attack (or Direct threat)

A threat to capture an enemy piece or give checkmate next move, if the opponent does not stop it. The first move of a 'Takes Takes Bang!' or 'Check Moves Bang!' combination always makes at least one direct attack, and often two!

Double attack

When one piece is attacked by two enemy pieces at the same time, or when one piece attacks two enemy pieces at the same time (for the latter, see also Fork).

Doubled/tripled pawns

Two/three pawns of one colour on the same file.

Endgame/Ending

The final phase of the game when few pieces are left on the board.

En passant

When a pawn which has just moved forward two squares from its original square, is captured by an enemy pawn standing immediately beside it. This capturing pawn then occupies the square behind the captured pawn.

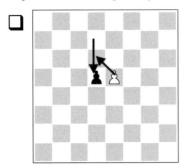

White captures the d5 pawn en passant

Exchange

1) When both sides capture pieces that are of equal value. Synonyms are 'trading' or 'swapping' pieces.
2) 'Winning the exchange' means winning a rook for a bishop or knight, a two-point advantage.

Exposed king

A king unprotected by its own pieces and, especially, its own pawns.

File

A line of squares from the top to the bottom of the board (e.g. 'the e-file').

Forcing move

A move that limits the opponent's options by making a concrete threat, such as mate or gain of material.

Fork

Attacking two or more enemy pieces simultaneously with the same piece.

Kingside

The board half on the white player's right (i.e. the e-, f-, g- and h-files).

Major piece

A queen or a rook.

Mate

See Checkmate.

Mating net

A situation where a king is attacked by enemy pieces and in the end cannot escape the mate threat.

Middlegame

The phase of the game that follows after the opening and comes before the endgame.

Minor piece

A bishop or a knight.

Open file

A vertical file that isn't blocked by one's own pawns, usually a great place to post the rooks.

Opening

The starting phase of the game.

Perpetual (check)

An unstoppable series of checks that neither player can avoid without risking a loss. This means that the game ends in a draw.

Piece

All chessmen apart from the pawns. In this book, mostly queen, rook, bishop and knight are meant, since many tactical motifs (sacrifices, for instance) cannot be carried out by a king.

Pin

Attack on a piece that cannot move away without exposing a more valuable piece behind it. Pins take place on a rank, file or diagonal.

Queenside

The board half on the white player's left (i.e. the a-, b-, c- and d-files).

Rank

A line of squares running from side to side (e.g. 'the third rank').

Sacrifice

When material is deliberately given up for other gains.

Skewer

When a piece attacks two enemy pieces that stand on the same rank, file or diagonal, and the piece in front is forced to move, exposing the one behind it to capture.

Square

One of the 64 sections on the chess board that can be occupied by a pawn, piece or king.

Stalemate

When a player who is not in check has no legal move and it is his turn. This means that the game ends in a draw.

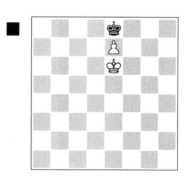

Black is stalemated

About the Author

American FIDE Chess Master Charles Hertan has been teaching chess to kids of all ages for more than three decades. He believes that kids' great enthusiasm and capacity for learning should be encouraged in every way possible, using humor, a personable style, and top-notch instruction that respects childrens' innate ability to appreciate the artistic beauty of chess.

Mr. Hertan authored the adult chess tactics book *Forcing Chess Moves* (New In Chess 2008), winner of the prestigious ChessCafé Book of the Year Award for 2008, and contributed a chapter to *The Chess Instructor 2009* (New In Chess 2008), a compendium for chess teachers, coaches and parents.
He also produced and edited a poetry book, *Dream Catcher: Selected Poems by Lynn Kernan* (Bunny & Crocodile Press, 2006), and also writes a regular tactics column for New In Chess Magazine.

He lives in Northampton, Massachusetts, and can be contacted at cehertan@rcn.com.

Index of Players

The numbers refer to pages.

A

Aagaard 20
Addison 34
Ahern 49
Almasi,I. 124
Anand 150
Anderssen 43-44, 89, 139
Apsenieks 18
Areshchenko 51

B

Bareev 108, 127
Barle 123
Barnes 88
Barros Lizcano 111
Barry 91
Bashilin 132
Bauer,R. 106
Baumber 72
Becerra Rivero 53
Becker 74
Beliavsky 120
Bernard 46
Bird 45, 144
Bjerring 80
Blackburne 92, 115, 148
Blanco Sanchez 59
Blass 122
Bocharev 24
Bodnaruk 145
Bogoljubow 82
Botvinnik 118
Bredoff 29
Broadbent 136
Bronstein 112, 126
Bruno,F. 103
Bryan 106
Buckle 143

C

Canal 49, 86
Capablanca 50, 76
Cardenas,E. 59
Carlsen 39, 83, 103, 125

Chapman 79
Chigorin 57, 129
Cochrane 38, 60, 108, 121
Colle 49

D

Danielian 77
Daniels 93
De La Bourdonnais 140
De Vere 62
Dean 95
Dehmelt 65
Del Pozo 8, 18
Diatsintos 44
Ding Liren 118
Dobos,O. 91
Dobrov 124
Dvoretsky 129

E

Eastwood 72
Ehlvest 105
Elianov 98
Elissalt Cardenas 37

F

Falcon Lugo 123
Farago,I. 66
Fedoruk 55
Fichtinger 74
Firman 51
Fischer 29, 34, 36, 47, 67, 87
Forintos 102
Friedmann 122
Frisk 51
Fritz 102

G

Gastein 100
Gelbfuhs 30
Genzling 137
Georgiev 145
Gheng 52

Gheorghiu 87
Gicin 96
Gilg 150
Gossip 35
Grant,J. 48
Griedner 138
Grigoryan,A. 24
Grünfeld 76
Gulko 94
Gunina 61

H

Hansen,T. 39
Hansson 102
Harikrishna 143
Harrwitz 109
Henrichs 111
Henriksen 132
Hertan 65
Hertneck 54
Heyl 62
Horwitz 109
Hradsky 51
Hübner 128
Hvenekilde 80

I

Ivanchuk 125

J

Jaenig 64
Jauregui 8, 18
Ji Dan 65
Johner 34

K

Kalashian 134
Kaplan,J. 112
Karnic,V. 95
Karpov 94
Kashlinskaya 141
Kasparov 25, 31, 38, 40, 54-55, 66, 68-69, 90, 96, 98, 105, 108, 120, 128, 145

Kieseritzky	44	Morawietz	48	**R**		
Knezevic	40	Morozevich	127	Rachels		38
Kolisch	100, 130	Morphy	104, 140	Radfar		125
Konnyu	54	Motoc	36	Raud		18
Korsus	48	Motoc-Mijovic	36	Recuero Guerra		146
Kortchnoi	79	Muhammad,S.	136	Reder		89
Kozel	96			Reiter,T.		125
Kozul	98	**N**		Robson		53
Kramer	67	Nagibin	141	Rodriguez Lopez		26
Kron,G.	99	Naiditsch	103	Rosenthal	57, 60, 144	
		Nakamura	80, 136	Rousseau	62-63, 121, 130	
L		Naumann	126	Ruck		83
La Rota	86	Neubauer	83	Ruy Lopez		53
Larsen	142	Neumann	27			
Lengyel	54	Neumann-Mayet	27	**S**		
Leonardo	53	Ngo Tan	99	Saint Amant		140
Levin	129	Nguyen Huynh Minh	146	Sämisch		76
Li Chao	127	Nielsen	61	Sarkar		111
Li Shilong	118	Nijboer	109	Schallop		52
Lilienthal	118	Nikolic,P.	69	Scharler		74
Llaneza Vega	64	Nilsson	132	Scheichenost		12
Loewe	42	Nimzovich	61, 150	Schiffers		35
Lupor	126	Nimzowitsch	34	Schmidt		123
Lushenkov	57	NN	104	Schmitt		134
Lushovsky	138	Novotelnov	139	Schrems		48
				Semprun Martinez		78
M		**O**		Serefidou		99
Mackenzie	42, 60	Obdrzalek	12	Severiukhina		61
Mahescandra	38, 108,	Olenin	57	Shamkovich		141
	121	Op den Kelder	111	Sharevich		145
Mareck	52			Shengelia		79
Marshall	50	**P**		Shirov		58, 150
Mason	42	Parnell	91	Short		68, 143
Matisons	86	Parr	136	Short,S.		49
Matlakov	88	Paulsen,L.	102, 116, 144	Shulman		80
Mayer,I.	62	Paulsen,W.	52	Sikharulidze		45
McDonnell	140	Peptan	131, 137	Simagin		139
McNab	20	Perez de Aranda	28	Simons		42
McShane	27, 79	Pert	72	Smyslov		47
Medley	45	Petrov	122	Sokolov,I.		27
Meitner	115	Pitschel	148	Solodovnichenko		109
Menchik	61, 74, 82	Podzielny	132	Stabolewski		66
Metger	124	Ponce Lopez	28	Stanley		63, 121
Michna	105	Popert	90	Staunton		60, 90
Miroshnichenko	77	Pozo Vera	78	Stefanova		131
Mitzka	89	Prieto Azuar	123	Stefansson		25
Mnatsakanian	100	Puller	92	Steinitz	30, 116, 138	
Mongredien	88	Purnama	120	Stripunsky		86

Strunsky	105	Uusi	134	Welling	126
Styazhkina	99			Williams	143
Svidler	82	**V**		Wyvill	89
Szabo,G.	139	Vaisser	61		
Szabo,M.	91	Van den Bersselaar	103	**X**	
Szen	43	Vassallo Barroche	26	Xu Jun	127
Sznapik	46	Vetoshko	96		
		Visier Segovia	141	**Y**	
T		Volokitin	84	Yakovich	83
Taimanov	36	Von Heydebrand und der Lasa		Yoffie	44
Tal	142		63	Yu Yangyi	131
Tarrasch	124	Von Jaenisch	69,	Yudasin	66
Thomsen	90		122		
Tiviakov	98	Vorobiov	58, 84	**Z**	
Tkachiev	82			Zaichik	45
Topalov	31	**W**		Zaitsev,A.	100
Torres Samper	37	Walker	93	Zhang Xiaowen	78, 148
Treybal	76	Wallenrath	69	Zhang Zhong	120
		Wang Jue	148	Zhao Xue	78
U		Ward	72	Zhou Weiqi	65, 131
Ulko	88	Weissgerber	134	Zukertort	129, 138